Getting **through**

TEACHER'S BOOK

by John Meredith-Parry and Lorraine Weller

Edward Arnold

© John Meredith-Parry Lorraine Weller 1980

First published 1980
by Edward Arnold (Publishers) Ltd
41 Bedford Square, London WC1B 3DQ

Reprinted 1985

British Library Cataloguing in Publication Data
Meredith-Parry, John
   Getting through.
   Teacher's book
   1. English language — Text-books for foreigners
   I. Title II. Weller, Lorraine
   428'.2'4   PE1128

ISBN 0-7131-8014-5

Text set in Univers IBM by 𝒜 Tek-Art,
Printed in Great Britain by Spottiswoode Ballantyne Printers Ltd.,
Colchester and London.

Acknowledgements

The authors would like to thank the following people:
Robert Smith and Peter Fredrickson for their help on the computer
pages.
Dermot Flaherty for all the dedicated research that went into writing
the 'Ordering a Drink' flowchart.
The Evemy family for re-arranging their lives on several occasions.
Dick Weist for 'Lost on the Moon' and 'DUTS'.
And Peter Weller for all kinds of help.

The publishers wish to thank British Rail for information adapted
from '1979 Family Railcard Application Form' (page 37)

Contents

Introduction
Whatever you do – read this first!

The most important and relevant aspects of short courses are these.

- The students are on holiday.
- Their motivation is often low and always varied.
- Teaching resources can be limited.
- Staff and premises are hired for a short period.
- The teaching and activity load is high, so there's little time for detailed planning.
- Some staff are new to English as a Foreign Language teaching.
- You never know the level of the students until they actually arrive.
- The range of language ability within classes is often wide.
- Attempting to teach the students a lot of new language is unrealistic; better to aim at giving them greater confidence to use what they already know.

Although these points may appear to be negative and somewhat daunting, don't be put off. Here's the positive side.

- The students are on holiday, so classes tend to be relaxed rather than formal.
- Resources are limited, so you have to generate and produce a lot of your own material with the class, which is very rewarding when it works well.
- You are often teaching two or more different nationalities in the same class, and can therefore exploit the fact that they can only communicate with each other in English.
- You can take advantage of a wide teaching brief, unrestricted by exam considerations or strict course limitations.

The result is that a fully planned course which follows a detailed course book is not really practical for five good reasons.

- The students often have different educational backgrounds. This means that their abilities to cope with the different skills of speaking, listening, reading and writing will vary widely. You may find, for example, that a student who has been orally graded as intermediate, produces written work which is advanced. (This happens regularly with Japanese students.) Similarly, students who appear to be quite fluent orally are often unable to write a correct sentence.
- Your students will progress at different speeds and will arrive with different expectations.
- Most students study English the whole year round in their own countries, and are understandably reluctant to follow the same kind of book they use at home.
- Students in a holiday mood prefer to hop from one language point or topic to another, rather than follow the 'page a day' approach.
- Much of the success of short holiday courses depends on the ingenuity and flair of the teachers, who *have* to produce much of their own material to suit the needs of their students. A strict course book can work well for the experienced EFL teacher who knows exactly how and when to use it, but it can, unfortunately, undermine the inexperienced teacher who has neither the knowhow nor the confidence to use it in this way. If you are inexperienced in EFL teaching, don't be afraid to adapt your own skills and experience to the new situation. Some of the best lessons we've seen on short courses came from junior school teachers doing just that.

But teachers and organisers do need some guidelines and ideas to help with the actual teaching. None of us really like teaching in a vacuum or on a totally free, non-defined programme. It's also extremely hard work to *produce* a coherent course at the same time as trying to *teach* it. It was these considerations that led us to write this book, which isn't designed as a page by page, day by day course book. Rather, we hope that it will be an adaptable and stimulating supplement to existing materials.

The main features of *Getting Through* are:

- a flexible format, to enable you to work on similar topics in different ways with students

of differing language ability, if necessary.
- the design, which makes the student's book look interesting in its own right rather than being an interesting-looking text book. Graphs, photos, cartoons and maps are used extensively at all levels, with an emphasis on written text in the advanced section.

The Teacher's Book.
The material is presented in a way which will be easy to use if you do have to cope with students of differing language ability. The different levels in the student's book have been grouped together. In other words, page one of the Elementary level is followed by page one of the Intermediate level and then page one of the Advanced level which is followed by page two Elementary etc. We hope that you won't have elementary and advanced students in the same class, but a mixture of elementary and intermediate, or intermediate and advanced is not unlikely, especially on smaller courses.

Symbols.
Five different symbols which give an overall view of the 'shape' of a lesson are used. You will find an explanation of them on Teacher's Book page 3.

Supplementary material.
At the beginning and end of each section in the student's book there is material which is useful for the beginning and end of a course. If you wanted to work through the book page by page, this could certainly be done; but we think it is more likely that you will want to follow the book quite closely at first and then dip into different topics as the course progresses. The London section, for example, is obviously best used to precede a visit there.

The Symbols

Teachers' books are often hard to follow because it is difficult to get an idea of the overall *shape* of a lesson from text alone. We've devised some symbols which we hope will give this at a glance.

This is what the symbols mean.

You are the black circle in the middle, surrounded by your class. The semi-circle grouping is not essential but does have the advantage of letting the students see each other's faces rather than the backs of other students' heads! This part of the lesson is teacher-directed. You are taking the initiative, you are controlling the situation and the students are listening and responding to your questions and actions.

This represents work across the class from one student to another and a less dominating role for you. You are more of an adviser and prompter.

Students work on their own.

Students work in pairs. Think about pair arrangements in advance. Sometimes the best results come from putting a strong and a weak student together. At other times, strong with strong gets the best results. Change the pairs frequently.

Students work in small groups, numbers depending on your particular circumstances.

Grading

In order to grade students into the appropriate language levels, most organisations provide a written test and back this up with an oral interview. The main purpose of a short holiday course should be to activate what the students already know in terms of improving oral communicative skills. In view of this, the best that can be said of written tests is that they keep the students occupied while you get on with the more important job of assessing their oral abilities.

Here are some points you might like to consider before starting on a morning's grading session.

- Interview as many students as possible in one session because it becomes easier to get an overall view of the level once you have done five or six interviews.
- If you haven't got a local written test, use one of the 'Spot the Differences' on the Games, Jokes and Puzzles pages at Elementary and Intermediate levels. Or, ask the students to write down a description of their house and/or family at home.
- After setting this, look for students who are struggling in the first few minutes. These are most likely to be your low level ones, so extract them as soon as possible for their interview.

We suggest that the most likely divisions you will want to make are: Elementary, Intermediate, Fast Intermediate, Advanced. Our definitions of the levels are these.

Elementary
They can handle a simple structure, even if it is incorrect, e.g. 'They is sitting', and they can manage simple vocabulary: sit/stand/house/hand/head/watch.

Intermediate
They can handle simple structures correctly, e.g. 'He's talking', 'He's holding a telephone', 'I arrived in England yesterday'.

Fast Intermediate
They have a good knowledge of vocabulary and can handle several structures correctly, e.g. 'I've been here since yesterday', 'I've never been to England before', 'I'd like to visit Stonehenge'. They are easy to understand and can ask you questions.

Advanced
They can handle most structures with confidence. They have a wide range of vocabulary and are clearly at ease using the language. They are likely to initiate questions themselves.

As a rough guide, the answers to the following general questions should give you an indication of their level.

Elementary
Where do you live?
Which city are you from?
What time is it?

Intermediate
Did you have a good journey?
How did you get here?
Have you been to England before?

Fast Intermediate
How long have you been learning English?
What would you most like to do/see while you're here?

Advanced
What would you do if you won £50,000?
Would you like to live here for a couple of years? Why?/Why not?

Remember that some of the students may be shy, nervous and tired. This obviously affects their language performance, and what often happens is that once they have settled down into the course, their performance improves dramatically. Because of this, it is always better to grade too low and put students up after a couple of days than grade too high and have to put them down.

You can, however, go some way to alleviating their anxieties by your own behaviour during the interview. Sit *next* to them, rather than opposite across a large imposing desk. Say 'hello' and ask for their name. Give your first name. If they have already done some written work, look at it.

Look at them when you ask questions and *listen* to their replies.

Don't spend too much time on the preliminary questions, but if you want more material, say for borderline cases, we suggest that you use the back cover of the book and ask the following questions.

Elementary
What can you see on the table?
Where are these people?

Intermediate
What are these people doing?
Who do you think they are?

Fast Intermediate
What do you think the woman is saying to the man?
Why is the man looking at his watch?

Advanced
What can you say about the man's room?
Have you any idea who the woman behind the door is?
Can you describe her expression?
What could've happened?

Projects and interviews

Projects are notoriously difficult to do well. Students and teachers alike tend to be suspicious of them because they often sound more impressive and interesting than they turn out to be.

There is a definite place for this type of work on summer courses. We hope that these notes, based on our own successes and disasters, will give you some tips and ideas.

Justification of projects

If you're not entirely convinced of their value yourself, this will quickly be picked up by your students, so here are four points in their favour.

- Projects give *real* practice in asking questions, listening, reading and writing — something you can't get from books.
- Projects highlight the difference between written and spoken English — an area that is necessarily often neglected in the teaching of English in foreign countries.
- Projects emphasise the importance of correct intonation patterns. 'Can I ask you some questions?' said in an aggressive pattern is less likely to result in co-operation than a less grammatically correct question said with a polite intonation pattern.
- Projects, especially in their presentation stages, often encourage the less linguistically able students to come out of their shells because they get a chance to display other talents e.g. lovely handwriting, talent for drawing, background knowledge of the subject chosen etc.

Approach

A fairly firm, disciplined approach with specific guidelines and time limits works best. Give plenty of practice in the structures they will need if the project includes getting information from members of the public, for example:

'Could I ask you . . . ?'
'I'm trying to find out . . . '
'I'm doing a survey on . . .   Could you help me?'

Discuss ideas for projects with your class. Having decided on the topic, make sure the students have a sense of purpose and a goal. This could be an end result consisting of a display or presentation to other classes, and/or at a social end-of-course evening which their host families attend. Don't rule out giving prizes for the best work and to the hardest working students.

Ideas

A class, or whole course, magazine.

This provides a definite goal to work towards, helps make a fair amount of writing practice more motivating and provides the students with a keepsake of the course which they can take home and show their parents. (Be careful though; on one holiday course in Tunbridge Wells, a pretty innocuous little magazine brought howls of protest from Spanish parents because there was a reference to 'kissing' at a disco' L.W.)

Topics which have worked well for us include:
- first/last impressions of their holiday
- 'What Do You Know?' (an International Quiz page)
- sightseeing trips and comments on them
- music — record and concert reviews
- opinions on food
- crosswords
- cartoons (especially of the teachers)
- 'quotes' about the course.

Try to hand over to the students as much as possible of the editing, correcting and artwork. Get them to design the cover, for instance. Give yourself enough time to type and photo-copy or print the sheets. Magazines are hard work but you should find that producing one is rewarding for both you and your students.

Town surveys.

These are best done from the students' point of view as tourists in the area. Get them thinking about the kind of advice they would have liked to receive when they first arrived:

best shops, best snack bars and restaurants, good pubs and discos, and where all these places are; system of public transport, fares, availability, convenience; places of interest in the area; sports facilities and so on.

The results of their survey along with their comments can be put together as a guide for students coming to the centre the following year.

Mini-projects using local and national radio broadcasts.

Listening activities. Listen to *short* news bulletins from different stations. (As a rough guide, a three-minute bulletin usually provides about twenty minutes of comprehension work.) Use them individually, and then comparatively to show students the differences in content and presentation between the various stations, e.g. formal versus informal styles of speaking - illustrated by speed of speech, choice of words (do they use phrasal verbs or the more formal Latin root words: 'The bomb exploded'/'The bomb went off'?), use of contractions ('Mrs Thatcher is going to visit Russia'/'Mrs Thatcher's going to visit Russia'). Does the station use jingles to introduce and end the news? If so, does this make it sound less serious?

Listen to a short extract from a phone-in or quiz programme. How do different people express themselves? What words and phrases does the presenter use to control them?

Listen to some ads. Note the amount of information given within the specific time slot, and the different ways which are used to get the message across.

Reading activities. Use copies of the Radio Times to find out more about the B.B.C's national service. Can the students work out the differences between Radios 1. 2. 3. 4?

Use local newspapers to find out programming on local stations. Look at the names of some of the programmes: do they reflect particular local interests or issues?

Collect publicity material from local stations. Use this as the basis of a fact-gathering activity, e.g. target audience, peak listening times, prices of ads at different times of the day, services available to listeners.

Writing activities. Students can write to the stations with specific questions they need information on, perhaps coming out of their reading work.

Or they could write to ask for a request to be played for the school.

Use this opportunity to teach or revise the layout of a letter in English.

Speaking activities. If possible, get the students to participate in a phone-in programme. This always works well and they find it very exciting.

Encourage them, if you have access to a cassette recorder, to make their own radio programme. Decide, with them, on the format and time limit. They should arrange themselves in small groups gathering news from the local paper, rewriting and finally recording. Some can work on writing ads, the weather forecast, a recipe for the day, traffic news etc. Include a main news item, two or three other items and one or two local short stories, which should include interviews with the characters involved. In this way, most people in the class should get the opportunity to participate actively. Choose one or two students to act as co-ordinators — this will allow you to take a back seat and act only in an advisory capacity, and it forces the students to take on the responsibility for the finished programme themselves.

Interviewing local people.

A potentially disastrous activity — think carefully before embarking on it and take into account that local residents often resent the annual invasion of foreign teenagers. Done well it can, in fact, prove a good public relations exercise for your organisation by going some way towards disproving what the locals think!

Preparation for interviews.
● Discuss the idea with your students and get them to suggest topics. Write them on the board. Let them decide among themselves which they would prefer to work on.
● Ask for possible general questions, select the most appropriate and write them up on the board. Work out a general interview outline with the whole class, then suggest

that, in pairs, they work out their own in more detail.

- Practise ways of stopping people in the street: 'Excuse me . . .' 'Could I just ask you . . . ?' 'Would you mind answering . . .?' Encourage them to practise the questions and possible replies in pairs, swapping roles so that they each get the opportunity to ask the questions. Point out that specific questions are better than general ones, e.g. 'Do you think there's an energy crisis?' is easier to deal with, for lower level groups, than 'What do you think of the energy crisis?'
- Teach them to recognise some of the negative responses they will undoubtedly receive in reply to their opening gambits, for example:
  'No, I'm awfully sorry . . .'
  'I'd love to but I've got to catch a bus.'
  'I'm sorry, I can't right now, I'm in a hurry.'
- Remember to tell them not to stand too close to people — some nationalities have a disturbing (to the British) habit of standing on top of you when you're talking to them. This unnerves a lot of people and could ruin the interview.
- Ask the students to decide on the sample. How many people will they interview? Age and sex should be taken into account. Equal numbers of different groups should be interviewed.
- The pairs should work out the timing of their interviews and, helped by you, should cut out weak questions if necessary. They then go out into the street and complete the interview in the time which has been agreed.
- In class, they should collate results and present them in whatever form they think is best, e.g. graphs, text, some recorded material or a mixture of these.

Suggestions for interview topics.
- Visiting the local tourist office to find out numbers and nationalities of foreign visitors to the area.
- What English teenagers think of the entertainment and sports facilities in the area.
- Attitudes of English people to foreign visitors.
- Interviewing people about their jobs: vicar, postman, traffic warden, Mayor, newspaper/local radio reporter, hospital worker, teacher etc.

- Going to the local police station to find out what problems foreigners have in the area, and what crimes (if any!) they commit.
  Remember that if any of the projects involve interviewing specific people in specific places, two or three pairs of students all coming on the same day asking the same questions will be rather tedious. Avoid this by getting the students to do a variety of interviews. Also, a phone call from you, explaining the situation and asking for help from potential interviewees is not only considerate, but will smooth the way for your students.

LOOKING AROUND
Comparing costs

Look at these things.
How much do you think they cost?

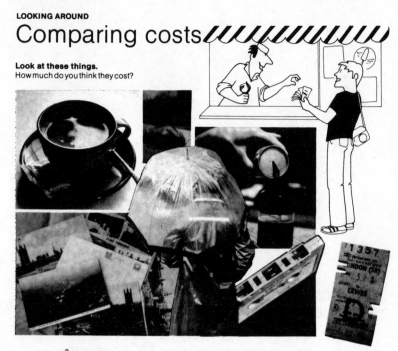

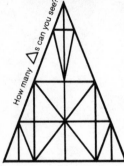
How many △s can you see?

NAPIS = SPAIN   What are the other countries?

RENFAC   RUPE   ANHIC   KERMAND

IYLAT   RAIN   PYGTE   LAVIYAGSOU

PAANJ   SWEYTGNEARM

MUIBLEG   CREEGE   DENEWS

RUTIAAS   DNALEAZWEN   ZIARBL

XEMOCI   OAOCMN   TWAUKI

6

Looking Around:

See note on phrasal verbs, **Extra 2**
Teacher's Book page 13.

Vocabulary and approximate costs:
(at time of going to press)

Cup of tea . . . 16p
Biro . . . 15p
Ice cream cornet . . . 30p
Postcard . . . 12p
Stamp to Europe . . . 13½p
Umbrella . . . £4.00
Plastic raincoat . . . £3.50
Can of Coke . . . 25p
Cassette tape . . . £5.50
Cheap day return
ticket (120kms) . . . £4.20

The countries are:

France Peru China Denmark Italy
Iran Egypt Yugoslavia Japan
West Germany Belgium Greece
Sweden Austria New Zealand Brazil
Mexico Monaco Kuwait

What about a quick quiz on the
capitals of some of these countries?

Triangles:

We think there are at least fifty:
Other shapes that could be taught:
square, circle, rectangle.

Aims	To establish the costs of common articles and currency exchange rates. To teach recognition of English coins and notes and their relative values. To teach 'How much does it cost?' To give the teacher an opportunity to assess further the students' oral competence. To provide activities for the students to do without teacher supervision.
Background	As the first day of a holiday course is usually quite demanding, we have included the activities at the bottom of the student's page so that you can leave them to work on their own for a few minutes if necessary.

Approach

With your help, students identify coins from their pockets. Make sure you have all the coins yourself plus a one and a five pound note. Remember, we tend to say 'p' more than pence.

Students identify as many of the photos as possible. Put vocabulary list on board. Show use of 'a' and 'an', e.g.   a cassette   an umbrella

Ask: **How much does a cassette cost, do you think?**
                        . . . cup of tea . . .
                        . . . postcard . . .
                        . . . etc.

Match correct prices with list of articles on the board. (See opposite.) Recognition and pronunciation of prices needs attention, e.g.   '15p', but 'one fifteen' for £1.15p.

Students, directed by you, ask each other the cost of articles:
'How much does a cassette cost?'
'About £5.50'.

Students compile a list of articles, showing their equivalent sterling prices in their own countries. They will need to know the *exchange rate*. Think about adding items like: films, L.Ps, glossy magazines, cinema tickets.

Put a list on the board, for example:

Article	Spain	Japan	Britain
a cassette	£2.60	£3.20	£5.50
an umbrella	£3.50	£5.30	£4.20

Students make comparative sentences using *cheaper/dearer*.

Extra

You may want to include a short interview session. See notes on Teacher's Book page 15.
     Teach and practise 'Could I have . . . please?' using a shopping context, plus the articles and prices on the blackboard.
     Teach 'change' and practise getting the right change.

Ask: **A film costs £3.40; you give the shop assistant £5, how much change do you get?**

LOOKING AROUND
Comparing costs and services

Start by writing down any number → add 7 to it → multiply your answer by 2 → now add 5

the result is ← always the same ← multiply by 3

Subtract the number you first wrote down ← divide by 6 ← Subtract 3

HOW MANY WORDS CAN YOU MAKE FROM 'GREAT BRITAIN'?

26

Vocabulary and approximate costs:
(at time of going to press)

Newspapers . . . 10-15p

Portable radio . . . £40

Portable black and white
t.v. set . . . £90
Portable colour set . . . £270

Second hand Renault 5 —
1977 model . . . £2,415
New Renault 5 . . . £3,800

Repairing heels on a pair
of shoes . . . £1.00
Key cutting service . . . 50p

Films, black and white
prints (36) . . . £1.30
and processing . . . £5.40
Colour transparencies . . . £4.60

Chimney sweep (each chimney)
. . . £3.00

Window cleaner (each window) . . . 30p

3 bedroom, terraced London
house . . . £35,000
(Give the price of a similar house in
your own area for comparison)

Ask:
WHICH OF THE ABOVE ARE *SERVICES*?

Words with four or more letters will
make this more difficult. Make a note
of your students' vocabulary level.

Probably better to do this in pairs.

You could also ask for a list of parts
of body and clothes shown here.

Aims	To establish the costs of common services and currency exchange rates.
	To allow you a chance to make a further assessment of the students' level of English.
	To provide activities for the students to do without teacher supervision.
Background	The first day of a holiday course is always busy. It's important to keep your students occupied, and at the same time to establish the right atmosphere and relationship with them. Look at the exercises and teacher's notes at the other levels and borrow extra ideas where appropriate. 'Intermediate' can cover a wide range and your main task is to assess whether your class is at the lower or higher end of the scale.

Approach Students identify as many of the photos as possible.

 Put vocabulary list on board. (See costs opposite.)

Ask students whether they think these items are expensive or not. How do they compare with their own countries?

The language they use will probably include the following:

'It's more expensive to develop photos in England than in . . .'

Note their responses to questions like the following.

Ask: **Do you have to buy a licence when you have a t.v.?**
Are newspapers delivered to your home in . . . ?
Do you have chimney sweeps/window cleaners in . . . ?

Assess the kinds of mistakes they make and use these as the basis for a later lesson.

Teach expressions of approximation, for example: 'I don't know how much it costs exactly — it could be . . . '

  — it might be . . . '

  — it's about . . . '

 Students write brief comparisons with their own countries in nationality groups where appropriate.

Extras

1. You could include a short interview session — see Teacher's Book page 15 for notes on this.
2. Phrasal verbs. Point out 'Looking Around' at the top of the page and mime searching for a lost article in the room; elicit/teach 'look for'.

   Mime walking down a road and suddenly shouting out to somebody; elicit/teach 'look out'.

   Mime holding a baby in your arms; elicit/teach 'look after'.

   Mime turning over the pages of a book and running your finger down the page, and then recognising and noting something; elicit/ teach 'look up'.

   Phrasal verbs seem to be neglected in the teaching of English abroad. To make up for this deficit, you might like to programme some in during the course. Choose a main verb such as 'get' 'take' 'come' 'let' and explore the different meanings that appear when prepositions are added, e.g. 'get on' 'get out of' 'get away from'.

   To test that your students have learnt them, write on pieces of paper the phrasal verbs taught, and give them out to half the class. Give the other half sentences like: 'I searched everywhere for my purse yesterday', i.e. containing the meaning of the phrasal verb. The students then have to go around the class and find their matching phrasal verb or sentence. Then, in pairs, they re-write the sentence using the phrasal verb.

LOOKING AROUND
Words at work

English spelling often confuses foreigners – and the British! Can you spot the spelling mistakes in these photos?

Here's part of a sign – can you complete it?

See if you can complete these words by reading their definitions:

C..L.P..NE
a transparent wrapping material

C.B...T
a kind of entertainment

H..I.O..E.
a kind of aircraft

I..L....B..
easy to burn

O...C..N
a maker of spectacles

Now why not have a go at writing your own? Try them out on another student.

Can you find two meanings in each of these advertisements?

46

Looking Around:

See note on phrasal verbs, **Extra 2** Teacher's Book page 13. At this level, you could also teach 'look up to' 'look down on'.

The mistakes are:

Business; bankrupt; acquired; facilities; handicapped; until; bicycle. Ask for meanings where relevant.

If they need help, tell them there's a clue somewhere in the book: (It's on Student's Book page 9)

The words are:

Cellophane; cabaret; helicopter; inflammable; optician.

Aims	To assess the level of the class further. To break the ice.
	To get the students looking at the language around them.
Background	At this level, you will probably find it useful to divide the class as often as possible in order to allow students to find and work at their own pace. Throughout this section, there will be a lot of project work with groups reporting back to each other. Much of your teaching is likely to be remedial. We aim to set up situations which will get the students talking. By noting down their deficiencies and inadequacies, you are then in a better position to correct and consolidate what they already know.

Approach Students interview each other for about ten minutes, and note each other's likes and dislikes, hobbies, ambitions etc. Afterwards they report back to the rest of the class on what they have found out about their partners.

 Students look at their books.
Group 1 looks at spelling mistakes.
Group 2 looks at the incomplete sign.
Group 3 looks at the meanings in the advertisements.
Group 4 looks at definitions.
   Each group looks at each section for 5 minutes maximum and then moves on to the next section.

 After 20 minutes, when each group has looked at each section, check answers with the whole class. Each group should keep a record of its score. (Answers opposite.)

Spelling mistakes.

Ask: **Do you have special spelling mistakes in English that you make all the time?**

Suggested short 'fun' test.

Ask: **What's the difference between 'it's/its?' And 'practice/practise' ? Can you spell: receive, sincerely, delicious, application, accommodation, piece, relevant?**

Incomplete sign.
Mime the actions of making a frustrating phone call. The first time you get a <u>crossed line</u>. Then the number is <u>engaged</u>. Then you <u>get through</u> but are <u>cut off</u> after five seconds.
   Elicit as much of the italicised vocabulary as possible. Revise the different tones you can hear on the phone: ringing, engaged, dialling, unobtainable.

Advertisements.

Ask: **What is the newspaper advertisement saying exactly? What do we call people who look in shop windows but don't go into the shop and buy anything?**   *Windowshoppers.*

 Ask the students to keep a record of wrong spellings which they see in ads and on shopfronts etc. Give a few examples: Fona Van/ Nappi Wite/Foto fast/Supakleen/Ansaphone/While U Wait.

Extra   *The Bag Lesson*
Take your bag or wallet, suitably sorted, into class and give out some of your personal effects. The students should work in small groups. They have to piece together as much information as possible from what you give them.
Suggested items: cheque book, season ticket, driving licence, credit cards, passport, a personal letter (written by you to yourself!)
They report back on their findings to the rest of the class.
   We have found this activity really helpful in establishing a good relationship with the class right from the start of the course.

GETTING TOGETHER
Family mealtimes

Which meal is this? What can you see on the table?

Saying 'Yes' and 'No' – politely!

Yes please

I'd love one
some

No thanks
I'm really full!

Would you like some more toast?
No thanks, but could I have another cup of coffee please?

7

Getting together:

You could teach extra phrasal verbs such as: get on, get up, get off.

Elicit some family relationships:

father	mother
sister	brother
grandmother	grandfather
aunt	uncle
cousin	

What about comparing *times* of meals between countries?
e.g.   What time do you have lunch?
         When do you have supper?

Aims	To teach some basic 'food' vocabulary. To teach polite requests and refusals.
Background	A lot of host families complain about the rudeness of the foreign students they have staying with them. Meal times can be particularly difficult because cultural differences and conservatism about food, combined with language inadequacy, can make students sound much ruder than they mean to be. It should be possible, even at elementary level, to teach some simple phrases which make what the students say more acceptable. The intonation of the phrases should be practised and the importance of 'please' pointed out.
Grammar note	Countables and uncountables, e.g. an egg/some scrambled egg, are often taught with food vocabulary. You will probably need to point out the difference between countables and uncountables, but on a holiday course we feel that the polite phrases and their intonation are a more crucial and realistic target for the students to aim for rather than 100% correct use of grammar.

Approach

Ask: **What did you have for breakfast this morning?**

Note answers on the board.
Check items in student's book, e.g. teapot, coffee pot, mug, bowl, etc.
Then teach: Could you pass the . . . please?
              Could I have the . . . please?

Students ask and answer questions using the list on the board.

Ask: **What's happening in the cartoon?**
       Elicit as much as possible.
Ask: **Would you like more toast?**
Students accept or refuse using the language given in their books.

Practice across the class.

Ask: **What's the question to 'I'd love one'?**
                       'I'd love some'?
     What can you say about 'one' and 'some'?

Draw on the blackboard.

Teach: boil/fry/scramble.
Mime how to boil an egg. Students try to put language to your actions:
Boil egg: Put some water in a pan; Put the egg in; Boil for three minutes; Take out; Put into an egg cup.

Get half the class, in pairs, to work out instructions for cooking a fried egg, and the other half to do the same for scrambled eggs.
Feed in vocabulary as necessary.

Extra

Families are likely to ask their students: 'What are you doing tomorrow/next weekend?' This future use of the present continuous for fixed arrangements is something which is useful to teach early on. We suggest that you deal with it in a straightforward way, just pointing it out and then checking with examples.

Ask: **What are you doing tomorrow?**

Board prompts: play/football; meet/friend; have dinner/cousin.

Family free time

Public holidays in England:

New Year's Day
Good Friday
Easter Monday
May Day
Spring Bank Holiday
August Bank Holiday
Christmas Day
Boxing Day

How many public holidays are there in your country?
Most European countries have more than Britain. Why do you think this is?

GETTING TOGETHER

Families

People used to work very long hours but nowadays families have much more spare time. We asked people what they did in their free time. Most of them had more than one interest! *(See chart below).*

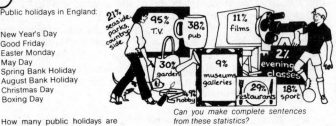

Can you make complete sentences from these statistics?

Interview another student and make a similar chart to show the amount of time spent on spare time activities.

As only 29 per cent eat regularly in restaurants, you can see that most English people eat at home. When you stay with an English family, you'll probably like most of the food you eat but sometimes, you'll want to say "no"! Here are some ways to say "no" *politely* when somebody offers you something you don't want or don't like.

I won't thanks…I'm putting on weight.
I'm on a diet.
I'm trying to lose weight.

Thanks very much but…I'm not really keen on…
I'm not very fond of…

But sometimes this isn't enough and some people will continue to offer you food. In this case, "Really, I couldn't" is a nice way to refuse a second time.

Use the new language to finish the dialogue. Here's the situation:
Mrs. Williams loves to see people eat. You're staying with her and you're on a diet. You've already lost ten pounds and you're determined not to put it back on!

Mrs. Williams : Do help yourself to more meat and potatoes.

You: ....

Mrs. W: On a diet! You could do with putting on a few extra pounds. I don't understand you young people...why do you all want to be so skinny these days? Have some more cabbage – that won't hurt you.

You: ....

Mrs. W: Aren't you? Well, I hope you've got room for a bit of pudding. I've made a lovely fresh cream trifle. You must try that.

You: ....

Mrs. W: Thank you very much, it's kind of you to say so. Now why don't you try this...it's English Cheddar and I don't suppose you've come across it before.

You: ....

27

Getting together:

You could teach extra phrasal verbs like:
get out of, get over, get on with.

Teach alternative ways of asking the questions:
How do you spend your free time?
What do you do in your spare time?

You could spend five minutes looking at the eccentricities of our sound/ spelling system:

weight   *height*
eight   sight
great   white
mate   bite

Can your students think of others?

Aims	To give some background information on family life in Britain.
	To generate language from the interpretation of an illustrated chart.
	To teach students how to refuse politely.
Background	See the points relating to 'rudeness' on Teacher's Book page 17. If the students are staying with families they should be encouraged to use mealtimes for conversation practice. This means that they will have to take the initiative sometimes. We have suggested some ways of doing this in the 'extra' section below.

Approach

 Students read the text.

 Exchange of information about different countries' public holidays.

 Students read the illustrated chart and make complete sentences.
Students interview each other and draw up graphs, OR compile a graph for the whole class and put it up on the classroom wall.

 Students read the new language. You offer individual students more food and they refuse, using the language given.

 Students practise offering and refusing.

 Look at the gap completion dialogue with the students. Note the idiomatic language: could do with/skinny/I hope you've got room for/you've come across it.
Encourage the students to speculate on the meaning of these phrases.

 Students fill in the gaps and practise the dialogue. Note the stress and intonation, especially:
'On a diet!'
'skinny'
'Aren't you?'
'You must try that.'

Extra

Mealtimes can provide a useful opportunity for conversation practice, and at this level students should be encouraged to initiate a conversation. Here are a few examples of mini-situations that you can use to elicit or teach opening conversational gambits. Point out that when in doubt, the British open a conversation by saying something nice.

1. **You come in, the family are watching television. What do you say?**

   This looks interesting, what's it about?

2. **You get some food, you don't know what it is. Find out.**

   Mm, this looks good, what is it?

3. **You're in a car with an English person. Start a conversation about the car.**

   This is a lovely/interesting/fast/comfortable car. How long have you had it?
   (Equally good, with different adjectives, for other possessions: bike, t.v. stereo).

4. **It's breakfast time. Start a conversation about the weather.**

   Isn't it a lovely day, do you think it'll stay like this?
   Isn't it awful, do you think it'll clear up?
   Have you heard the weather forecast yet?

GETTING TOGETHER

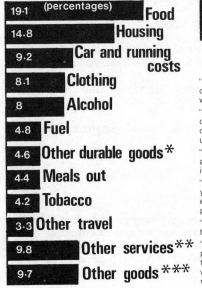

Family life
3 ways
of looking
at it

EXPENDITURE of income

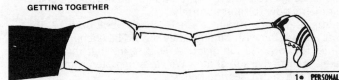

(percentages)	
19·1	Food
14·8	Housing
9·2	Car and running costs
8·1	Clothing
8	Alcohol
4·8	Fuel
4·6	Other durable goods*
4·4	Meals out
4·2	Tobacco
3·3	Other travel
9·8	Other services**
9·7	Other goods ***

1 • PERSONAL

DAVID SHOULD BE IN A HOME, NOT A HOME

David is a 3½-year-old, with sandy hair and blue eyes and we think that if you saw him you would agree that he should not be living in a Residential Nursery where he has been for the last 2 years. He should be growing up in a family. He seems a bright child, unusually imaginative and he loves being read to and playing make-believe games. He sometimes retreats into himself and sucks his thumb and at other times he is boisterous and rather restless. He is confused and angry that he is not living with his mother. Because of his mother's difficulties she will not be visiting David in the foster home, but his social worker will take him occasionally to see her. We expect David to remain in the foster home for the rest of his childhood, but as he may take some time to settle we are prepared to pay an enhanced boarding out rate of up to £40 per week. David should be the youngest child by at least 3 years because he needs a lot of individual attention.
If you would like to find out more about David and live in London or the Home Counties, contact ... ... Great Tr...... ster ... ...

"...sometimes I dream about being an orphan. I could do anything I wanted, I wouldn't have to worry about hurting my parents...."

"The family is just another way for the State to control the people – only it's more subtle. Instead of using direct force to make people conform – it uses emotional blackmail...."

"...I love my family a lot, I just wish they'd learn to accept me as an adult equal and stop trying to interfere in my life all the time...."

"I hate visiting my family – it's all so false. There you are, stuck in a room with people you don't even like – but you're supposed to love them. I prefer my friends; I chose them myself...."

"My hairstyle, my clothes, my books, my boyfriend. Why do my parents control all this...?"

"Family life is based on exploitation. I exploit my parents for food, clothing and pocket-money – they exploit me by expecting me to be what they want in return for food, clothing and pocket-money. It's a vicious circle...."

47

Can they think of other vicious circles?
What about: inflation; population growth in poor countries.

Do British people smoke less/more than people in their own countries. Have they noticed any 'no-smoking' areas here?
Does anti-smoking advertising have any effect?

Getting together:
You could teach extra phrasal verbs like:
get down to, get up to, get by on.

Explore some of the ways we describe hair:
colour: sandy/ginger/streaked/ greying/bleached/dyed/ mousey etc
texture: frizzy/curly/wavy/straight/ permed/dry/greasy etc

* e.g. carpets, suites, music centres.

** e.g. dry cleaning, laundry, window cleaning, plumbing.

*** e.g. cosmetics, entertainment.

Aims	Presentation of new vocabulary to describe different kinds of family life. Extended speaking practice through role play.
Background	It is quite likely that some of your students come from broken homes. This is a delicate area and some students may be reluctant to discuss this page on a personal level. On the other hand, it may prove to be another useful ice-breaker, especially if you offer some information and views on your own family background or situation. It's always useful to have an idea of your students' backgrounds and this page will provide you with a chance to get to know them all a little better.

Approach

 Students look at and interpret the graph.

Ask for comments in relation to their own families.
   Elicit/teach the following:
separated/divorced/widowed/unmarried mother/one-parent family/ broken home/to foster a child/to adopt.

Students read the text 'David should be in a home, not a home'.

Suggested questions to check comprehension:

Ask:　**Where's David living at the moment?**
What's the colloquial word for a 'residential nursery'?
Who does he play games with?
Can you give other words for 'bright' and 'boisterous'?
What do you think a social worker's job is?

Students read the quotes on family relationships.

Ask for comments.

Role play

We call this type of role play 'minimal' because only the bare facts and an outline of the situation are given. It is up to the students to provide the context.

 Divide the class into three groups. These represent the social worker, the foster parents and David's mother. The social worker group can be twice as large as the other two groups. Each character has a clearly defined objective:

Mother	You want David back. Justify this objective.
Foster Family	You don't want to give David up. Justify this objective.
Social Worker	You have to decide what to do with David. Justify your decision.

Give the groups 10 minutes to decide on their arguments/tactics. The Social Worker group should decide on the kind of questions it is going to ask the other groups. It should also decide on its attitude towards the claims of natural vs foster parents. It should consider David's improvement, or lack of it, in the last 3 years.
　A representative from each group presents the collective justification. You should arbitrarily call on other group members to take over the presentation at any stage. The Social Worker group can interrupt at any point with questions. At the end, the Social Worker group discusses the various arguments and finally gives its decision to the other groups. You can feed in further information in order to direct the activity at any stage of the proceedings by passing notes on slips of paper to the groups. They have to work these in during the course of their part of the discussion.

Extra

Ask the students to read through the ad. again, then ask them to write a similar description of themselves.

LOOKING CLOSER
Differences

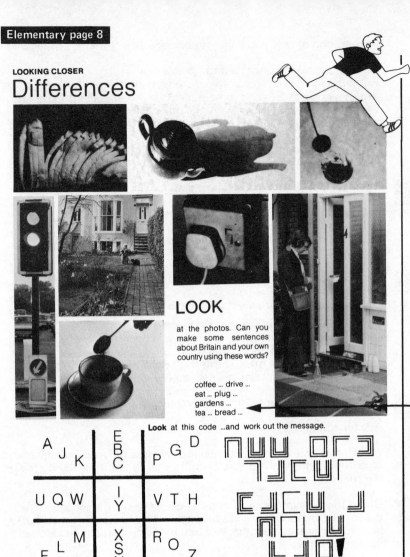

Consider changing a plug in class and explaining the colour codes.

The sequence of traffic lights is:
Red; Red and Amber; Green; Amber; Red.

LOOK

at the photos. Can you make some sentences about Britain and your own country using these words?

coffee ... drive ...
eat ... plug ...
gardens ...
tea ... bread ...

Such as:
We don't have sliced bread in . . .
English people drink a lot of tea, we drink coffee.
You drive on the left, we drive on the right.

Look at this code ...and work out the message.

The message is:

See you later. Have a nice day.
Here's the code:

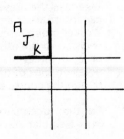

8

Aims	To revise the pronunciation of the English alphabet. To focus the students on some of the differences between Britain and their own countries. To teach 'I like' and 'I don't like'.	
Background	Students invariably compare Britain to their own countries. On this page, we want to exploit this situation by pointing out some of the smaller, everyday differences such as: electric plugs and sockets, instant coffee, bathplugs, and the people who deliver things to our doors.	
Approach	Ask: **What can you see in the photos?**	

Teach/revise main items of vocabulary.

Students, in pairs, produce sentences from cues in book.

Exchange of sentences. Each pair writes one sentence on the board while the other students look for mistakes and correct them where possible.

Draw two faces on the board:

Ask: **What do you like in Britain?**
What don't you like in Britain?

By questioning 3 or 4 students you can build up a table of likes and dislikes, for example:

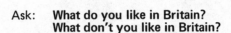

	Coffee	Tea	Bread
Anna	✓	x	x
Mehdi	x	✓	x
Juan	x	x	x

The other students can then make sentences practising the 3rd person singular from the table, for example:
'Anna likes coffee but she doesn't like tea'.

Ask: **Can you work out the coded message?**
Here's a clue.

On the board draw: A is ⌐J|

Decoding competition. (Answer opposite.)

Point out sound groupings of letters, e.g. AJK.
Write particular problem letters on the board, and practise them, e.g. a/e e/i j/g v/w

A game of 'Hangman' is good for consolidating letter sounds. You think of the first word but then hand over to the students. Play for fifteen minutes maximum.

Extra Students work out their own coded messages and give them to other pairs to work out.

LOOKING CLOSER

Lewes–a county town

County town of East Sussex
80 kms from London
12 kms from Brighton
Pop. 14,250
Early Closing: Wed.
Winter min. temp. 2°C
Summer max. temp. 21°C

Norman Castle built at end of 11th century: 2 mounds, 2 towers.
Museum includes stocks and whipping post.
Famous Battle of Lewes in 1264.

Tourist Centre
187 High St. Tel.6151
Hospital Tel. 4153
Police Tel. 5432
Fire Tel. 3333

Hourly trains to London (Victoria) 55 mins.
B.R. Tel. 4618

New Eastgate shopping centre

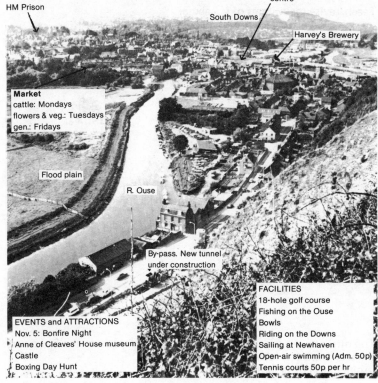

HM Prison

South Downs

Harvey's Brewery

Market
cattle: Mondays
flowers & veg.: Tuesdays
gen.: Fridays

Flood plain

R. Ouse

By-pass. New tunnel under construction

EVENTS and ATTRACTIONS
Nov. 5: Bonfire Night
Anne of Cleaves' House museum
Castle
Boxing Day Hunt

FACILITIES
18-hole golf course
Fishing on the Ouse
Bowls
Riding on the Downs
Sailing at Newhaven
Open-air swimming (Adm. 50p)
Tennis courts 50p per hr

28

Try this quick true/false quiz. Your students should be able to do it with books closed if you do the main lesson first. Ask them to jot down the answers.

1. The train journey from Lewes to London takes an hour.   (F)
2. It costs 50p an hour to use the open air swimming pool.   (F)
3. The shops close early on Wednesdays. (T)
4. Harvey's Brewery makes very good bread.   (F)
5. You can buy tomatoes at the market on Fridays.   (T)
6. The battle of Lewes was in 1264.   (T)
7. Lewes is 18 kms from London. (F)
8. The museum is in the castle. (F)
9. The shopping centre was built recently. (T)
10. Bonfire Night is on November 4th.   (F)

Aims	To help the students understand abbreviated information.
	To show them how to compile and present similar information about their own towns.
	To practise extended speaking.

Background
During the first few days of a course, students often find it difficult to express their opinions and talk about their experiences. This is a natural part of the linguistic 'tuning-in process' and a lot of teachers notice a vast improvement in their students once they are three or four days into the course. This page is designed to do two things: first to present general information about a specific town; and second, to give the students a chance to use the method of presentation to describe their home town or city. We find it works well because it is a subject about which the students always have something to say. They are in the position of knowing more than you and so there is a reason for them to speak. Your job is to guide them towards discovering a form for their content.

Approach

 Students look at the photo and read the information.

 Suggested questions to help students work out the meanings of some abbreviations.

Ask: **Where is Lewes?**
How many people live there?   (explain 'pop'.)
Does it get very cold in winter?   (explain 'min/max temp'.)
Where's the tourist centre?

 Students think of questions to ask each other. Use blackboard cues if necessary, for example:
1264?
How long/journey/London?
When/castle/built?

 Check students' comprehension of:
Market + abbreviations
Brewery
By-pass
Facilities

Ask the students to group the information under headings. Let them try to work out the headings themselves, for example:
— Geography — position/climate/population
— History — important events/monuments
— Industry
— Tourist attractions
— Sports facilities
— New developments
— Useful information for tourists

 Where possible, students, in groups, work on compiling mini-presentations of their own towns, either in visual or written form, using the headings already discussed. This should be followed by oral presentation to the rest of the class. If most of your students come from the same town, they can divide into smaller groups, each to work on one or two of the above headings in more detail.

Extra

Project
Compiling a foreign students' guide to the area. See notes on setting up this type of project on Teacher's Book, page 6.

LOOKING CLOSER

You could use the drawing to pick out some of the following vocabulary. From left to right: sneakers/pleated skirt/low-heeled shoes/bald/checked shirt/V.-necked sweater/wedge-heeled sandals/helmet.

Exploiting tourists

What to wear
sunglasses
comfortable shoes
casual jacket with large pockets

Where to go
seaside promenades
tourist traps
the London Underground
airports
banks and *bureaux de change*

Who to look for
people with two or more cameras
tans
souvenir T-shirts/shorts
bulging wallets
dictionaries/phrase-books

How to steal
A crude and dangerous method is to use a sharp knife to cut or slit handbags. It's more subtle to pick pockets. All you need is lots of practice!

What to sell
Be guided by the weather. **If it's hot,** sell ice-creams and chilled drinks. **If it's wet,** sell umbrellas. **If it's cold,** sell hot dogs.
Always add 50 per cent to the advertised price – tourists don't usually notice. If you're given five pounds, always give change for one. It often works! Do the same with 50p pieces. Talk quickly.

— Ask the students to explain . . .

Some other methods:

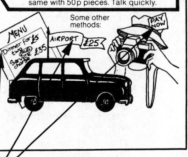

48

Ask the students to explain . . .

Aims	To teach the language of giving advice using positive and negative structures. To warn students about some of the ways they might be persuaded to part with their money in tourist 'traps'
Background	A lot of exploitation of unwary tourists goes on during the summer. This page may help to put your students on their guard. On the other hand, it's not unknown for students to get involved in shoplifting, for example. They should be warned from both points of view. Your local police force will usually be very happy to send a policeman to talk to your students. This page would be worth doing before such a visit.

Approach

 Books closed. Ask your class to think of ways in which foreign visitors are exploited in *their* countries.
Where are the favourite places? How is it done?

 After 10 minutes maximum, the students should check their ideas against those in the book and exchange ideas between groups.

 Divide the class into four groups:
1. Clothes　**2.** Position　**3.** Targets　**4.** Methods

Each group has to prepare a short presentation on the points listed in the student's book, giving reasons for their inclusion. Encourage them to add any further points of their own.
Introduce the following phrases to each group *separately* on pieces of paper:

Group 1　You're recommended to . . .
　　　　　Make sure you don't . . .

Group 2　You'd be better off . . . -ing . . .
　　　　　Be careful not to . . .

Group 3　Keep your eyes skinned for . . .
　　　　　Under no circumstances . . .

Group 4　As long as you . . . you'll be all right.
　　　　　Whatever you do, don't . . .

Tell each group that they have to use each phrase at least once in their presentation to the other groups. They should elect two students from each group to be the presenters. Help them with any phrase which is difficult but don't let the groups overhear each other's phrases. Note that each negative phrase forces the students to produce their own ideas and language.

After about 10 minutes, hold a petty criminals' meeting in which each group presents its findings.
The students who are listening should not only note the conclusions but, *more importantly,* should identify the phrases which were introduced by you. After each presentation, they should say what these phrases were, and give their meanings. If they can't do this, get the students who used the phrases to teach them to the rest of the class.

Students work out what's happening in each of the cartoons.

Extra

Students organise and write their own guide: 'How *not* to get ripped off while on holiday'. If you decide to do a magazine, include this in it.

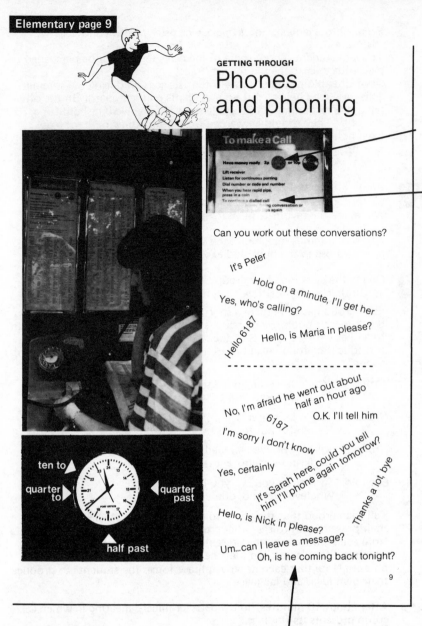

GETTING THROUGH
Phones and phoning

Now 5p!

Can they guess what to do to continue a call?

Ask the students to find a phone box after school and complete the instructions.

Can you work out these conversations?

It's Peter

Hold on a minute, I'll get her

Yes, who's calling?

Hello 6187

Hello, is Maria in please?

- -

No, I'm afraid he went out about half an hour ago

6187   O.K. I'll tell him

I'm sorry I don't know

Yes, certainly

It's Sarah here, could you tell him I'll phone again tomorrow?

Hello, is Nick in please?

Um...can I leave a message?

Oh, is he coming back tonight?

Thanks a lot, bye

9

ten to
quarter to
quarter past
half past

The order is:

1. Hello 6187
   Hello, is Maria in please?
   Yes, who's calling?
   It's Peter
   Hold on a minute, I'll get her

2. 6187
   Hello, is Nick in please?
   No, I'm afraid he went out about half an hour ago
   Oh, is he coming back tonight?
   I'm sorry I don't know
   Um . . . can I leave a message?
   Yes, certainly
   It's Sarah here, could you tell him I'll phone again tomorrow?
   O.K. I'll tell him
   Thanks a lot, bye

N.B. We say 5 past, but 4 *minutes* past.
Ask the students to say the time shown in as many different ways as possible, i.e. 21 minutes to 12
          11.39
          23.39 (at night).

This second conversation will probably take the students at least 15 minutes to work out.

Aims	To teach the students how to use a pay phone.
	To practise basic language used when making phone calls.
Background	It is possible to borrow phones from the local G.P.O. Alternatively, children's toy phones can be used. Putting students back to back when practising phone dialogues makes the situation more realistic.

Approach

Mime making a call from a phone box.

Ask: **What am I doing?**

Main vocabulary and stages:
lift the receiver
dial the number
put the money in the slot when you hear the pips.
Check student comprehension by calling out single words to individual students, who then put the word into an instruction. The other students should mime the action, for example:
lift/number/pips/dial/slot/receiver/hear

First jumbled dialogue
Note special language:

'It's . . .'   'Who's calling?'   'Hold on'.

Students practise saying dialogue before moving on to second dialogue in different pairs. The second one is a lot more difficult and is intended more for passive recognition than for active reproduction. Therefore it isn't necessary, or even advisable, to try to get the students to say it fluently.
(Answers opposite.)

Extra

Pronunciation of phone numbers, including codes. Useful numbers, e.g. Operator, Directory Enquiries, Emergency.

Give the students some 'Don't speak, listen' numbers without telling them what they'll hear, for example:
Bedtime Stories
Dial a Disc
Recipe
Speaking Clock
Weather Forecast.
Students should report back the next day on what they heard.

Use the dialling code book as a source of scan reading material. Students can find out the various call charges at different times and for different distances, for example:
How much does it cost to phone Madrid for 7 minutes, at 8.00 a.m.?
How much time do you get for £1 if you phone Paris at 6.30 p.m.?

GETTING THROUGH

Phoning and posting

— Now 5p!

The phone

How would you say these numbers:

01 353 7891
0892 5311
0226 6444

If you want to ring these numbers from a call box in Piccadilly Circus, what exactly do you dial?

Complete this telephone conversation:

Michelle: Hello 4137

Brian: . . . .

M: Yes. Is that Brian? How are you? I haven't seen you for ages.

B: . . . .

M: Oh, I'm sorry to hear that. I didn't know. Are you better now?

B: . . . .

M: Well, I'm going away for the weekend but I'm not doing anything on Friday night.

B: . . . .

M: That'd be great. I'd love to.

B: . . . .

M: Could you make it a bit later – I don't usually get in until about 6.30.

B: . . . .

The post

Have you ever thought about what you can and can't send through the post? For example, the British Post Office doesn't allow red packets or envelopes or "any other colour likely to cause strain on the eyes of the Post Office staff. Cards, labels or envelopes should preferably be white. There is no objection to other colours (except red) provided that the shades are not (glaring, vivid, dazzling) in effect, or too dark". *(Post Office Guide)*

In the *Post Office Guide*, there is a long list of things that you can't send through the post to certain countries. You can't send books or photographs to Poland, Japanese shaving brushes to Uganda, communist literature to Peru, or old boots and shoes to South Africa.

Here are some other things which certain countries don't allow to be sent in by post. Look at the clues and see if you can match the thing to the country.

Bolivia   China   Switzerland   Mexico   Greece
Sweden   Russia   Denmark· Saudi Arabia

Watches   Soap   Playing cards   Toothpaste
Horoscopes   Sugar   Chewing-gum   Pork
Honey

Clues

A large and timeless country.
Paradise for Latin American dentists.
There's no future in cuckoo clocks.
They're sweet enough in Stockholm.
Forget poker – just enjoy the Ouzo.
Banned by religion.
Vodka is preferred to this Western habit here.
"To bee, or not to bee?" Not in Hamlet's country.
Wash well before you visit this high-up capital city.

29

Elicit sequence of making a phone call by using the photos. You could link with Student's Book page 9.

You can't send:

watches to China
toothpaste to Mexico
horoscopes to Switzerland
sugar to Sweden
playing cards to Greece
pork to Saudi Arabia
chewing gum to Russia
honey to Denmark
soap to Bolivia

Here's another gap filling conversation you could try:

Mr. Taylor: . . . .

P.C. Williams: Could I speak to Mr. Taylor please?

Mr. Taylor: . . . .

P.C. Williams: It's P.C. Williams from the police station here.

Mr. Taylor: . . . .

P.C. Williams: No, it's not about your dog this time later sir! It's about your wife.

Mr. Taylor: . . . .

P.C. Williams: Well, your neighbours have been complaining about the noise.

Mr. Taylor: . . . .

P.C. Williams: Oh I see, sir. In that case, if you could let your neighbours know – I'm sure they'd understand.

Aims	To illustrate the difference between 'can' for ability (i.e. 'I can swim') and 'can' for permission (i.e. 'Can we swim here?').

To teach the pronunciation of telephone numbers.

Background

In Britain, the Post Office is owned by the state and is divided into two sections. One is telecommunications, which covers telephones, telex etc. and which is highly profitable. The other is the parcels and letters business, which runs at a loss. A lot of people think that this state monopoly should be broken up.

Approach

The Post

Students' books closed. Dictate the first paragraph by reading the whole of it first, then sentence by sentence. Students write it down. They check the text by looking in their books.

Check and extend vocabulary, e.g. illustrate the differences between packet/carton/bag/box.

Students group themselves into a circle. Address one student.

Ask: **Can you swim?**

Round the circle, students ask each other questions with 'can'. If they all follow the same pattern, i.e. use 'can' for ability only, use question cues to get the other type, e.g. smoke/classroom?

Different types of questions should be noted in two columns on the board, one for ability and one for permission (but don't label them as such yet).

So, if a student asks 'Can you speak Russian?' put 'Russian' in one column. If a student asks 'Can you smoke in class?' put 'smoke' in the other column. Put requests like 'Can you open the window?' in a third column.

Continue around the class and then ask your students to tell you the differences in the meaning of 'can' in the two or three columns you've built up.

Students read the rest of the text and match countries and articles. (Answers opposite.)

The Phone

Teach your class how to pronounce phone numbers in English.

Put them into pairs to work on completing the dialogue. They should pay special attention to pronunciation, stress and intonation. Ask a few of the pairs to act their dialogue out to the rest of the class.

Extra

1.   If they enjoy completing the dialogue, see opposite for another one for them to try.

2.   See Teacher's Book page 29 for mini phone projects.

GETTING THROUGH
Phone or post?

Please hold on, there is a long delay!

0--------4---4---4---4---8-------3--2-
0--------5----CLONK.......BRRR-BRRR.....
BRRR-BRRR.... BRRR-BRRR........CLICK."Hoozat?.....
Sorry, is that you Mum?........ Airdrie 420?....Where?....
.... Scotland!.... Sorry, wrong number. I'd better get off the line
quick...............I said.......Oh, never mind, bye."....CLICK.
BRRRRRRR.0--------- 4---4---4---
8-------

Wouldn't a letter say it better? *Basildon Bond*
by John Dickinson

"Hello Mary?...It's me...Roger.
...You know, Roger....How
are you?...Long time...I'm well
...Been a few weeks, hasn't it?
...Listen, I'm sorry about that
party...Don't you remember?
That party...Oh never mind...
And see you soon too...Maybe
one day....Yes, who knows?
...Goodbye...Goodbye Mary
...Goodbye."

Wouldn't a letter say it better?
Basildon Bond
by John Dickinson

"Hello Joyce?...Who's that?
...Oh, Peter, Hello Peter. Could
you fetch your mummy please?
...It's your auntie Carol. How do
you know it's your auntie Carol?
Because I said so, Peter.....Now
could you fetch?....Yes I'd love to
hear your nursery rhyme, Peter
....And you want me to hear
your alphabet too?..............
....................Well done,
Peter.......Now could you fetch?
...And your two-times table,
as well?"

Wouldn't a letter say it better?
Basildon Bond
by John Dickinson

You could also revise: bring, take,
lend, borrow.

Note:

dad	daddy
mum	mummy
dog	doggy

Point out that these forms are
normally used either by, or when
talking to, children. Have your
students come across any more?

49

Aims	To teach some colloquial phone language. To give practice in coping with the unexpected. To point out some of the differences between spoken and written English.
Background	These are authentic advertisements for Basildon Bond writing paper. They were part of the 1979 advertising campaign and appeared in the national press and on the London Underground.

Approach Divide class into three groups, each to look at one ad. They should work out what is happening in each case, supply their own reasons for the phone call, state who is speaking to whom, and provide suitable responses for the person on the other end of the phone. Divide large groups again into working groups of three or four.

 Students exchange their findings and act out the complete dialogue.

 Use these dialogues as a basis for an exploration of the differences between the spoken and written word. For example, contractions like isn't/won't/she'll/it'll are forms which are fine in speech and informal writing, but inappropriate in business and other formal letters; similarly, omitting auxilliary verbs is all right informally, as in 'Do you want a drink?'/'Want a drink?', 'Have you had a nice time?'/'Had a nice time?', 'It's a lovely day isn't it?'/'Lovely day, isn't it?'
   Check that they know the different kinds of salutations and endings for letters:

Dear Sir/Yours faithfully
Dear Ms Jones/Yours sincerely
Dear Sally/love

 Students write a letter from Roger to Mary apologising for what happened at the party. They should invent this themselves. End by inviting her to another party next weekend.

Extra

Unpredictable phone dialogues
Put the students into pairs, back to back. Give instructions, written on a card, to each student. They shouldn't know what is on each other's cards and should react to the situation as it happens. Here are some examples:

Pair 1
Student A   Phone your boyfriend John/girlfriend Jane. Ask him/her to a party.
Student B   Your name is not John/Jane. You got out of the bath to answer the phone.

Pair 2
Student A   Phone your friend. Ask him/her out for a drink.
Student B   Agree to go out for a drink. Ask where to meet, then suddenly remember a previous engagement.

Pair 3
Student A   Phone your girl/boy friend. Ask her/him out for a meal.
Student B   After your *ex* girl/boy friend's behaviour at last week's party, you never want to speak to her/him again!

These work best if you can record them. Failing that, make notes of any language errors or more colloquial language that could have been used, and go over the conversations later, getting the students to practise the new items.

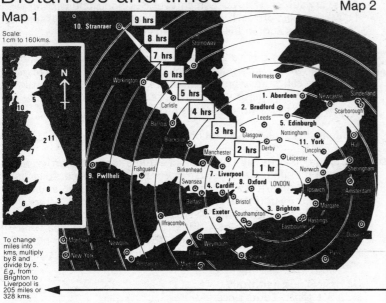

GETTING AROUND
Distances and times

Map 1

Map 2

Scale:
1 cm to 160 kms.

9 hrs
8 hrs
7 hrs
6 hrs
5 hrs
4 hrs
3 hrs
2 hrs
1 hr

To change
miles into
kms, multiply
by 8 and
divide by 5.
E.g. from
Brighton to
Liverpool is
205 miles or
328 kms.

Doing simple sums is a good way to
get your students understanding and
practising English numbers.

LOOK at MAP 1 and complete the sentences:

Edinburgh is about 645 kms north of London.
Cardiff........................... London.
Oxford .... York.
Liverpool......................... London.

Edinburgh is further from London than Oxford is.
Brighton is nearer to London than Norwich is.
Cardiff....... Liverpool....... Edinburgh is.
York.......... Brighton.......... Oxford is.

NOW LOOK at MAP 2

It takes three hours to get from London to York.
.... London to Edinburgh.

10

What do MAPS 1 and 2 show?

Look at MAP 2. What can you say
about the travel connections
between London and Wales, and
London and Scotland?
Why do you think they are different?

Look at both maps and compare
the following places:

Edinburgh/Bradford
Fishguard/Amsterdam
Pwllheli/Madrid
Oxford/Brighton
Paris/Aberdeen

Map 1 — Answers:

Cardiff is 240 kms west of London.
Oxford is 320 kms south of York.
Liverpool is 320 kms north-west of
London.

Cardiff is nearer to Liverpool than
Edinburgh is.
York is further from Brighton than
Oxford is.

Map 2 — Answers:

It takes three hours to get from
London to Edinburgh.

Maps 1 and 2 — Answers:

The connections between London
and South Wales are very quick.
Between London and North Wales,
they're much slower. You can get
from London to Scotland very
quickly.

Industry is the main reason for quick
connections. North Sea oil has been
very important in Scotland —
especially Aberdeen. The coal and
steel industry is important in South
Wales. There is no industry in North
Wales; it's a tourist centre, so the
connections are poor.

Aims	To give the students a better idea of the geography of Britain in terms of distances and travelling times.

Aims

To give the students a better idea of the geography of Britain in terms of distances and travelling times.
To practise pronouncing British place names.
To revise prepositions.

Background

Reading maps will be an exercise with which most of your students are familiar and which they usually enjoy. We have noticed that many students are unaware of distances in Britain, and few know the locations of major towns and cities. The travel map on the right will seem strange at first, but when compared with the left-hand map, we hope that it will lead to some interesting deductions about travelling in Britain. The average travelling times include travel by air, on commercial flights where possible. So, in terms of time, Madrid is 'nearer' to London than Fishguard is.

Approach

Students look at Map 1 and complete the sentences while you put up a rough map of the local area on the board, marking the school and places like the railway station, bus station, police station, sports centre etc. Make sure it includes: traffic lights, zebra crossing, cross-roads and roundabout.

Ask: **Can you make sentences about the map on the board?**
The Post Office is north of the railway station. The Police Station is nearer the school than the Post Office is.

How long does it take to get from the school to the Post Offi
Continue with 3 or 4 examples, marking the times on the board.

Similar questions across the class. With the students' help, add more things to the map: public lavatory/nearest pub/café, etc.

Students ask and answer questions on their own for 2 or 3 minutes

Say: **Look at map 2.**
Ask a question about London and Brighton.
How long does it take to get from London to Brighton?

Similar questions across class.

Students compare maps 1 and 2 and answer the questions on the page (See opposite).

Go through their answers all together. You may like to ask them to look at Exeter and Penzance. What can they say about these places, and what do they think about travel in Cornwall? (You could tell them that people who live in Cornwall say that a Cornish mile is longer than an English mile as it always takes so much longer to travel in Cornwall because of narrow winding roads!)

Extras

1. Nationality groups work on simplified time maps of their own countries and then give mini-presentations to the rest of the class. They should include facts about the travel times and the reasons for them — especially the anomalies, like Cornwall.
   With single-nationality classes, divide them into small groups and give them the same task. Compare results.
2. The Picture Dictation on Teacher's Book page 120 would be another useful extra.

GETTING AROUND
Cheap travel connections

HOW TO CHOOSE YOUR RAIL TICKET and save money.

Here are some ways to save money when travelling by train.

Awayday Return

This ticket can save you up to 45 per cent on the standard fare. You have to travel after the rush-hour period in the morning, Mon - Fri, but can travel at any time on Sat, Sun or Bank Holidays.

Big City Savers

There are special low-priced tickets on certain trains. You have to book in advance – at the latest by 1600 the day before you travel. It's first come, first served and numbers are limited, so don't delay.

Fare Deal Bargains

These are for longer trips. In addition to Standard Tickets, which can be used on any train, there are

30

different fare bargains to help you on special trips:

WEEKEND RETURNS are available for most journeys over 60 miles. Go on Fri, Sat or Sun, and return the same weekend on Sat, Sun or Mon, and save up to 35 per cent on the standard fare.

MONTHLY RETURNS are available for most journeys over 65 miles. Go any day and return within a month. Monthly returns save you up to 25 per cent on the standard fare.

Family Railcard

For £10 this railcard allows you to take a second adult and up to 4 children for only 50p each, when you buy single, return or Awayday return tickets. You can travel as often as you like until the card becomes out of date.

Which is the best ticket to buy if:

1. You're planning a day trip to visit an old friend. You don't mind which day of the week you go.

2. You want to go to Scotland for a week leaving London on a Friday.

3. You are married and have a child aged 12. The three of you want to visit your sister for the weekend. She lives at the seaside, about 80 miles away.

4. You have a business appointment at 10.00 a.m. in Manchester. The rail journey there will take you about two hours.

5. You live in London and you want to go to Bristol for a week. You don't mind when you travel.

Answers:

1. Awayday Return.
2. Monthly Return.
3. Weekend Return, or Family Railcard.
4. A Big City Saver might be possible here if you went on the right train. Otherwise, you've got to buy a standard ticket.
5. Monthly Return.

Extra train vocabulary:

first class/second class/running late/
running on time/delayed/cancelled/
slow train/fast train

Luggage vocabulary:

shoulder bag/overnight bag/suitcase/
rucksack etc.

Aims	To give a sample of the kind of language found in travel brochures.
	To practise scan reading for extracting specific information.
Background	Travel bargains change so often that it is virtually impossible to keep up with them. We suggest that you use this page as a lead in to the latest publicity material from British Rail. Students are often unaware of the savings that can be made by buying certain tickets. Also we strongly advise working in the ideas from the Elementary or Advanced levels, depending on the level of your class.

Approach Students read information on AwayDay Return and Big City Savers.

 Ask: **When's the morning rush hour?**
What's the maximum you save with an Awayday Return ticket?
Can you buy a Big City Saver on the day you travel?

Check comprehension of 'standard fare'.

 In pairs, students read the rest of the text and work through the questions.

Check answers with class as a whole. (See opposite).

Extra

Filling in forms
The form below, or a similar one, should be obtainable from any local railway station. Useful language, found in a wide variety of application and order forms, includes: non-returnable/please tick appropriate box/block capitals/debit/surname/forename/Ms.

Family Railcard application form

Please complete using BLOCK CAPITALS and send this coupon to British Rail Family Railcard, P.O. Box 28, York YO1 1FB.

Delivery of the Family Railcard will normally be completed within 21 days. Cards may be used from 17th June onwards until 29th February 1980.

  i)   Name of adult applicant(s)
Surname MR/MRS/MS   Forenames

_____

ii) Surname MR/MRS/MS   Forenames

_____

Address

_____

_____

_____

Tel No. Home   Date

_____

Signature of adult applicant(s)
i)_____

ii)_____
Your Name and Address for return Label (Block Capitals please)

_____

_____

_____

GETTING AROUND
A Londoner's map
of Britain

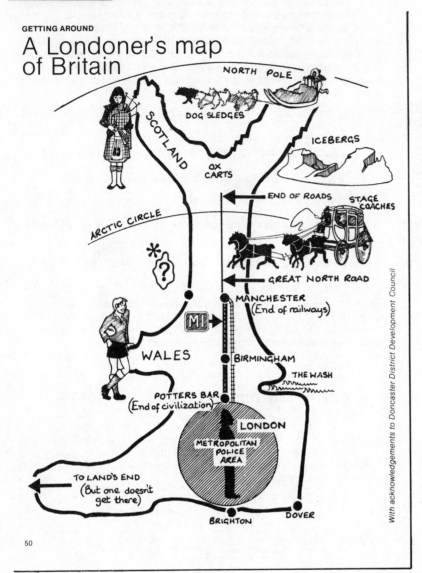

Idioms connected with 'ice':

the tip of the iceberg
to break the ice
to be snowed under

With acknowledgements to Doncaster District Development Council

50

* Isle of Man

Answers:

Scotland's in the Arctic Circle; it has very poor travel connections.
Law and order only exist in the area stretching from Brighton to Potters Bar.
The railway system and the M.1. end at Manchester. There are no roads in Wales or the south west.
You never get to the south west.
It's extremely cold in Scotland and the people wear strange clothes and play an odd instrument.
Wales has no roads, the men play rugby.

Aim	To give students an idea of the geographical prejudices that exist within the British Isles.
Background	This map first appeared in a book called 'Mental Maps', which showed how different people view their environment and its relationship to other areas. All your students will have an image of Britain in their minds. It is the differences between these images that we want to exploit on this page.

Approach

 Books closed. Divide the blackboard into three boxes and ask three students to come up to the board and draw an outline map of Britain. If possible, arrange it so that they can't see each other's, but the rest of the class can see them all.

Ask the class positions of:
London/the most popular area for EFL schools/the main industrial areas/the coldest area/Manchester.

Mark in their answers on the maps, using all three if there is a lot of controversy.

Books open. Students look at the map. Ask what they think it shows.

 Ask them to write down what the map tells them about:
Scotland/law and order/transport/south west Britain/the climate/Wales.

 Go through their answers. (See opposite).

Write the following notes on the board and ask the students to put them into sentences about the map:
terminus/inaccessible/out on a limb/un-named/road and rail network/uncivilised.

Check some of the sentences with the class as a whole

Get the students to devise a mental map of their own country, including reasons for the attitudes shown. Alternatively, and better with multi-lingual classes, have them work on mental maps of each other's countries.

Extra

Ask the students to show the map to their families and note their reaction to it. If they laugh — why?

You could also link this page with Student's Book page 10.

IN THE NEWS
Local papers

Under a Tenner

KITCHEN cabinet, 6ft x 3ft, £8 — Hailsham 842434.
STICKS of plumbers metal, £1 per 1lb stick. — Herstmonceux 2046.
WOODEN garden table, 48in long, 21in wide, very good condition, £3. — Herstmonceux 2046.
WARDROBE, 2ft 6in, £5. — Lewes 6778.
BEDSTEAD, 2ft 6in, wood ends with good clean mattress, £8. — Lewes 6778.
WHITE drop-side cot with mattress, £9 — Tel Seaford 890084.
TEN strong packing cartons, 5 cubic feet capacity, 50p each. 2 Buckhurst Close, South Malling; callers pm weekdays.

YOU DRINK WE DRIVE
H. & H.
PRIVATE HIRE
061-761 6286-p

Education & Tuition

ENGLISH for foreign students, full-time and part-time classes, examination courses, call in and see us. — Oakhurst School of English, 59 High Street, Lewes. Tel Lewes 71358.

Pick Your Own
Bramleys for storing 4p
Lord Lambournes 4p
Worcesters 4p
Laxtons for storing 4p
Coxs 8p
Cheaper for 30lbs
OPEN 9 to 7 daily
Pittlands Farm
Churn Lane, Horsmonden
Tel: Brenchley 2773
Opposite Brenchley Village Memorial Hall, take road one mile over crossroads to Castle Hill Stores, turn left down hill at De Claire Public House. Bear right at T road bottom of hill into Churn Lane (Marden Road). Carry on ½ mile — Pittlands is second farm on left.

BUNN'S SECOND HAND DEALERS!!
Will buy your washers, fridges, cookers, display cabinets, bookcases, tables, dining suites, all kinds of furniture, cycles, prams, playpens, cots, stereos, record players etc. Full or part house clearances. For a quick pleasant deal:
RING "BUNN'S" — Day 764 8439. Evenings 764 6333.
—z

BURY GROUP OF CHARITIES: Good as New Shop, 146 The Rock. Open Monday, Wednesday, Friday and Saturday. Goods required. — 764 2006. Will collect.
—z

JUMBLE SALE at The Salvation Army, Moorgate, Friday, May 18th, at 6.30pm. (Jumble gratefully received on Wednesday, May 16th, between 2 to 3.30pm or 6.30 to 7.30pm).

Personal

UCKFIELD Town Council Town Hall, annual meeting in Town Hall, Tuesday, March 27, 7.30. TA31

LOST & FOUND
LOST; Gold watch of sentimental value on the 8am 481 bus from Tottington to Bury on Saturday, May 12th. If found please ring 761 7184.
—p
LOST: White budgie, Monday, May 14th, Fishpool area. — Tel: 764 0155.

SUICIDE? Deepair? Telephone the Samaritans in confidence day or night East Eastbourne 35556, Hastings 436666, Tunbridge Wells 32323.
TA35

British local newspapers give you useful information. Some are weekly and some are daily. They give you local news, tell you about local entertainments and have advertisements like these.

What's a tenner?

Draw a map to show someone how to get to Pittlands Farm from Brenchley Village Memorial Hall. Start like this:

HALL

You want to sell a table and four chairs. Who do you ring?

You're going to a party. You want to have a good time and don't want to drive home. Who do you phone?

What happened on the 8.00am bus to Bury?

Who do the Samaritans help?

Who wants you to call in and see them?

11

Answers:

A £10 note is called a tenner.

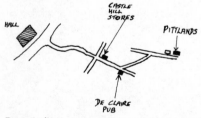

Bunn's (Ask students for night and day numbers).
H & H private hire.
Somebody lost a gold watch.
People with big problems.
The Oakhurst School of English.

Aims	To practise scan reading.
	To give students the confidence to make use of the information available in local newspapers.
Background	Students often worry about understanding the meaning of every word they read. This page shows them how to pick out essential information and work out meanings from context.

Approach

Ask: **What kind of information do you find in a newspaper?**
Use a copy of the local paper to illustrate the vocabulary if necessary: home news/sports news/t.v. and radio information/cinema and theatre information/advertisements.

Students work through the ads and questions in the book for 20 minutes maximum. Keep teacher interference to a minimum to force students to work together (Answers opposite).

Extras

1. *Game*
Split the class into two teams. Give each some copies of the local paper.
Ask: **What time does the film at the Odeon start?**
Which page is the T.V. guide on?
In their teams, they should work out and write down similar questions to ask the other team. A student from Team A asks Team B a question. After 1 minute she asks a particular student for the answer. A correct answer scores 2 points, an incorrect one 0 points. If the student doesn't know the answer, the rest of the team can decide on it together, but they score only 1 point for a correct group answer.

2. Teach/revise local geography and directions by taking a detailed look at the Entertainments page. Students choose where they want to go at the weekends. They then ask and answer questions on where the various places are, for example:
A   Where are you going this weekend?
B   I'm not sure — to the disco at the Elizabethan Barn, I think.
A   Where's that?
B   In the High Street, next to the station.

3. Use the diagram on Page 51 in the student's book. Ask the students if they know the names of any English newspapers. Put them up on the board. You'll need to teach 'left-wing' and 'right-wing', but will find that most classes are interested in learning about the political positions of the British press.

4. Using copies of your own local paper, set a similar exercise to the one on the student's page opposite, later in the course.

IN THE NEWS

Local radio

Until some years ago the BBC was the only radio company allowed to broadcast in Britain. Today it no longer has this monopoly. 19 independent radio stations have been opened and there are plans for more.

Advertising pays their operating costs and they aim to provide a truly *local* community service. The BBC has also opened local radio stations.

Both services broadcast music programmes, quizzes phone-ins, discussions about local events and regular news bulletins. Peak listening time is between 7 and 9 in the morning but late-night programmes are also popular. Most of the commercial stations broadcast round the clock. But why has local radio become so popular – especially with younger listeners? How is it different from national radio?

Here are some examples of ways in which local stations have helped their local communities:

In the hot dry summer of 1976 there was a serious fire in the North Yorkshire countryside. Radio Cleveland broadcast an appeal for volunteers to help the firemen and got 150 within half an hour.

After a mining disaster Piccadilly Radio sponsored a concert in Manchester. £7000 was raised and was given to the miners' families. Every day the station also gives details of credit cards that have been lost or stolen in the area. This service is very useful for local shopkeepers.

Radio Tees has a regular spot in which details of lost pets are given to listeners.

When several people in Middlesborough became ill with polio, Radio Tees provided information about vaccination centres.

In the farming area of Cumbria, Radio Carlisle broadcasts information about orphan lambs, or sheep whose lambs have died, so that farmers can contact each other.

Some areas have a high proportion of immigrants. BRMB radio in Birmingham has a weekly programme of music, news information and ads for

Independent radio companies

Asian listeners broadcast in Hindustani.

In Ipswich, there were serious floods in 1976 which caused huge power failures. Radio Orwell provided vital information on the air and helped prevent a major disaster.

What other help do you think a local radio station can give to an area?

One of the most popular and successful commercial stations is Capital Radio which began in 1973 and now has over 5 million regular listeners in the London area. Of Londoners in the 15-24 age-group, an incredible 4 out of 5 tune in to Capital every week. Here are some reasons why.

Its Jobfinder service invites young jobless people to drop into the office or phone 01-636 3261. They are given details of job opportunities and the service is free.

If you're looking for someone to share your flat, Nicky Horne's Tuesday evening programme takes details by phone and publishes a free list on Wednesday for people who are looking for accommodation.

If you've lost touch with old friends or relations, write to Michael Aspel and he'll read out your message in the "Where are you now?" part of his Tuesday morning programme.

Open Line on Wednesdays gives similar help on the air for people who phone in with emotional problems.

Swop Shop gives you the chance to exchange anything for anything by phoning on Thursday mornings around 10.00 a.m.

1 Belfast

2 Birmingham

3 Bradford

4 Edinburgh

5 Glasgow

6 Ipswich

7 Liverpool

8 London

9 London

10 Manchester

11 Nottingham

12 Plymouth

13 Portsmouth

14 Reading

15 Sheffield and Rotherham

16 Swansea

17 Teesside

18 Tyne/Wear

19 Wolverhampton /Black Country

31

Quick true/false test to do after the main lesson. Students should jot down the answers.

1. The B.B.C. controls commercial radio in Britain.   (F)
2. Swansea Sound is a Scottish radio station.   (F)
3. Most commercial stations end their programmes at midnight. (F)
4. There are 19 independent radio stations in Britain.   (T)
5. London has 2 commercial stations.   (T)
6. Younger listeners prefer the B.B.C. to commercial stations.   (F)
7. Birmingham's local radio is called BRBM.   (F)
8. Piccadilly Radio is a London station.   (F)
9. Peak listening time starts at 7.00 a.m.   (T)
10. Capital Radio first began broadcasting in 1972.   (F)

| Aim | To give an introduction to local radio, which will provide a base for wider project work. |
| Background | Although this page can be used as a lesson in itself, local radio provides a rich source of authentic listening, reading and writing material which is usually highly motivating. We suggest that you set aside some time over the week to explore these different areas. |

Approach

Elicit as much information about British radio as possible. Your students should be aware of the following facts at the end of the general discussion.

The BBC is the only *national* radio station in Britain. It gets its money partly from T.V. licence fees — £34 a year for colour t.v., £12 for black and white — and partly from a Government grant.

It broadcasts four national services — Radio 1, 2, 3, 4.

The BBC also has *local* radio stations.

Commercial radio is not connected with the BBC.

The different commercial radio stations are not connected with each other.

They are all local stations.

Their money comes from advertising.

Students look at the map and identify their local commercial station.

Students read the first three paragraphs while you put key words and phrases on the board:
monopoly/broadcast/quizzes/phone-ins/news bulletins/peak listening time/round the clock

In pairs, students try to work out the meanings from the context.

Check answers with the class as a whole.

Students read the examples of ways in which local stations help listeners.

Ask: **How often does Radio Tees broadcast details of lost pets? What can you say about the weather in parts of Britain in 1976? How does Piccadilly Radio help local shopkeepers? Where is BRMB Radio and what two languages does it use?**

In pairs, students spend five minutes thinking of other ways local radio stations could help listeners.

Compare suggestions with the class as a whole.

Use the reading comprehension on Capital Radio as the basis of a quiz which will give students practice in forming questions.

Split the class into two equal groups. Ask them to read the text and then write one question each to ask their opposite number in the other team. Students should work together as a group to ensure that they don't duplicate questions. Stress that the questions must be grammatically correct. Teams will lose one point for each incorrect question asked. Seat the teams in two rows, facing each other. The first members of both teams should ask and answer their questions. Score two points for a correct individual answer. If a student cannot answer, the question is given to the whole team who must discuss it and elect one member to give the answer. One point only for a correct group answer.

Students should be allowed to scan the text before answering, but set a strict time limit: 30 — 45 seconds.

Extra

See Teacher's Book page 7 for extra ideas.

IN THE NEWS
The British Press

Daily newspapers

LEFT ——————————— RIGHT

Morning Star
circulation:
38,533

Daily Mirror
3,670,812

Guardian
403,088

Financial Times
207,228

Times (pre-suspension)
293,787

Daily Mail
1,967,869

Daily Telegraph
1,538,180

Daily Express
2,412,025

Sun
3,802,636

Star
948,903

Figures April to September 1979

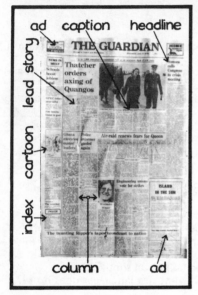

What would you expect to find inside these sections of a newspaper?

| Financial | Overseas | Classifieds |
| Home | Arts | Diary | Stars |

Newspaper headlines use English in a special way. They are usually short and dramatic. Look at these headlines and work out how they have been shortened:

Man bites dog

DC 10 in bomb blast

Cloud over oil talks

Ex model weds MP

Queen to visit China

Mr C jets to summit

Princess quizzed in nude-killer hunt

Look out for:
Shortened words
Missing words
Use of tenses
Word changes
Exaggeration
Dramatic usage

Headlines in full:

A man has bitten a dog.
There has been a bomb explosion on a D.C.10 aircraft.
A big problem has arisen at an oil conference.
A woman who used to be a model has married a Member of Parliament.
The Queen is going to visit China.
Mr. C. has flown to a meeting of heads of state.
A princess has been interviewed by detectives who are looking for someone who killed a woman who was found naked.

51

| Aims | To give information on the political background of the British Press. To show specialised vocabulary and syntax in newspaper headlines. |
| Background | The Daily Mirror, The Daily Star and The Sun have a very low vocabulary load, which the majority of English eight-year olds would know. However, their use of it is highly idiomatic and even advanced foreigners have difficulties interpreting many of their stories. From a linguistic point of view, the Daily Mail seems to be the easiest one for students to start on. |

Approach

Take in copies of as many different national dailies as possible. Have at least *one* per two students.

The students have their books closed.

Ask: **When there's sun and rain, what do you get?** *Rainbow.*
What do you see in the rainbow? *Colours.*
What do we call these colours? *Spectrum.*
What does that mean? *Full range/choice.*
What about the political spectrum? *Left and right wing.*

Draw on the board:

Ask: **What do we call the position in the middle?** *Neutral/unbiased.*
Name a British newspaper.
Where do you think it is in the political spectrum?

Let the students speculate and then write it up in its correct position. Build up the positions of the other papers in the same way until you have a chart looking something like the one in the student's book.

Students open their books and look at circulation figures. Ask for the highest and lowest. Do they know what 'pre-suspension' means? Do they find the figures surprising? If so, why?

Students read the annotated front page in their books and relate it to their own paper.

Students answer the question on sections of a newspaper and check their answers in their own newspapers.
Students look at and discuss headlines in their books and identify: shortened words/missing words/tense use/word changes. (See opposite).

Choose a main story which appears in all papers and discuss the varying headlines and treatment given to it by the different papers. Look at: length/vocabulary/style.
Finally, ask class to give a description of a typical reader of their paper. Help them by advising them to look at: ads/letters/the Editorial.

Extras

1. A few years ago, The Times ran an ad which just said 'Even if it's grim, we'll bare it'.
   See if your students can work it out. Ask who they think 'we' refers to — list possibilities on board. Ask if 'it's' and 'it' refer to the same thing. Can they guess what 'it' is? List possibilities on board.
   Give the meaning of 'grim' if necessary. Ask them the meaning of 'bare' in this context (*expose*). Can it be spelt another way? Now can they work out the 'hidden' meanings in the sentence?
   a) Even if the news is very bad, we, The Times, will expose it.
   b) Even if the news is very bad, we, The Times, are strong enough to bear it. (in other words; we'll still publish it).
   Finally, teach the expression 'Grin and bear it'.
2. Interview a local reporter on his/her job.

SNAPSHOT SESSION
Photo-stories

Can you make a story by connecting at least *five* of these photos?

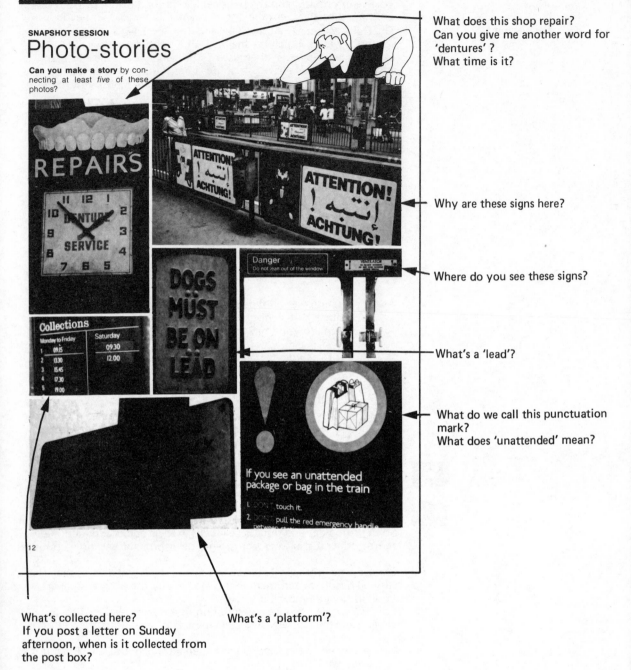

What does this shop repair?
Can you give me another word for 'dentures'?
What time is it?

Why are these signs here?

Where do you see these signs?

What's a 'lead'?

What do we call this punctuation mark?
What does 'unattended' mean?

What's collected here?
If you post a letter on Sunday afternoon, when is it collected from the post box?

What's a 'platform'?

Aims	To allow the students a freer and more imaginative use of English and help them to use their passive vocabulary.
	To give practice in extended writing.
Background	Elementary students are usually kept on a fairly tight rein as far as their use of language is concerned. We feel that one attractive aspect of short courses is that fluency and confidence can, for once, take precedence over correctness.

Aims
: To allow the students a freer and more imaginative use of English and help them to use their passive vocabulary.
To give practice in extended writing.

Background
: Elementary students are usually kept on a fairly tight rein as far as their use of language is concerned. We feel that one attractive aspect of short courses is that fluency and confidence can, for once, take precedence over correctness.

Approach

: Ask general comprehension questions about the photos. (See opposite.)

Students should try to put together five or more photos to make a story; they should write it down and then tell it to the rest of the class. If they can't connect five, let them do the activity using fewer. Set a time limit of around 15 minutes to keep motivation high. Allow as much language as possible to 'fall out' of the exercise and keep a note of what the students say. You may be surprised at some of the vocabulary they know. Concentrate on noting errors of structure which can then form the basis of later lessons.

Extras
: Photos cut from magazines provide a good source of language work.

1. Give out photos showing people talking and ask the students to provide some dialogue.

2. Back a photo on to some stiff card. Flash it at the class and ask them what they saw. Flash it again and continue until they have built up a verbal description. Then show it properly and discuss the differences between the actuality and what they thought they saw. This is a good ten minute warm-up activity for the beginning of a class when students are still drifting in and you don't want to start on your main activity.

3. You can do a similar warm up, or more extended question practice session, by showing the class the back of your photo and then getting them to ask you 'short-answer' questions from which they can deduce the content of the photo, eg. 'Is it an animal?'.

SNAPSHOT SESSION

A day out

In the same way that New York and Paris don't represent life in America and France, so London doesn't truly reflect life in Britain. A country town is more typical of our way of life.

Imagine you are spending a day with a friend in such a place. These photos are a selection of some of the signs you might see.

3. You see this notice in a shop window. What's it about?

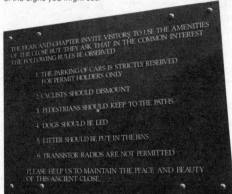

1. When you arrive, you head for the Cathedral; in the grounds, there's a sign:

a) What do you need if you want to park your car here?
b) Are bicycles allowed here?
c) What must dogs wear?

2. After seeing the Cathedral, you go to the town centre. On the way you see a message on a tree.

a) Would the owner give you anything if you found this cat?
b) What's the cat wearing?

32

4. You both feel peckish so you decide to have an early lunch. This pub menu catches your eye.

a) What do you think a Fork Lunch is?
b) What kind of food could you order on a Saturday?
c) If you had Chicken and Mushroom Pie with Beans, followed by French Bread and Cheddar and a cup of coffee, how much would your bill be?

5. After lunch, you stroll down to the Castle.

a) How much do you have to pay?
b) Where do you buy the tickets?
c) Two reductions are offered. What are they?

> Have you noticed anything odd about this page? *E.g., where* did you spend your day?

Answers:

1. a) A permit.
   b) Yes, but you can't ride them.
   c) A lead.

2. a) Yes.
   b) A blue collar.

3. A shooting competition. (Ask students what you can buy at the farm and if the people will shoot live pigeons.)

4. a) The kind of food you can eat without using a knife.
   b) You would only have a choice of 3 dishes from the menu.
   c) £1.32p.

5. a) 25p for the castle, or 40p for castle and museum.
   b) Barbican house museum.
   c) One for children and one if you buy a ticket for the castle and museum together.

01 is the London telephone code but the castle is in Lewes, Sussex.

Aims	To give practice in scan reading and guessing meaning from context.
	To introduce new idiomatic vocabulary.
	To give practice in agreeing and disagreeing.
Background	This page should provide students with an interesting way of picking up basic information on various aspects of life in Britain from the authentic material in the photos.

Approach

 Check and practise, if necessary, the structures we use when agreeing and disagreeing:

I think the answer is . . .
No, I don't agree, I think it's . . . because . . .
This must be the right answer . . .
It can't be this one . . .
What do you think?
It could well be . . ., because . . .
It might well be . . ., because . . .
It can't possibly be . . ., because . . .

Then put the students into pairs and leave them to answer the questions for a maximum of 30 minutes.

Check answers with class as a whole. (See opposite.) Ask for explanations of the following: to head for/to feel peckish/to catch your eye/to stroll.

Extra

Camera project
Most students bring cameras with them and are interested enough in photography for you to capitalise on this quite easily. Teach the vocabulary needed for using a camera and the actual taking of pictures. If possible, take in an unloaded camera so that the students can open it and look inside. Draw a simple camera on the board, label the parts as follows.

1. Viewfinder
2. Shutter release
3. Film rewind knob
4. Lens
5. Aperture

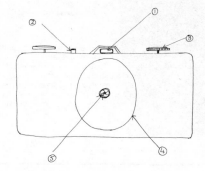

Then 'load' the camera with a black and white film. Check the 'film speed' and number of 'exposures'. 'Wind the film on'.
Ask the students to tell you how to take a photo:
-- Look through the viewfinder
— Check the aperture
— Focus the lens
— Take the photo by pressing down the shutter release.
Encourage the students to use a film collectively. Get it developed quickly, then discuss and mount the photos. Useful vocabulary could include: over exposed/under exposed; in focus/out of focus; background/foreground.
You could also suggest that the students design their own quiz, based on the one in their books. This could be mounted, with questions, and other classes could be brought in to do it, perhaps during the last week of the course.

SNAPSHOT SESSION

A night out

Brighton, as you probably know, is a famous holiday town on the south coast of England. Young visitors like it because there's lots of night-life and easily available information.

Look at the round picture. This guide can be bought in most local newsagents. What would you ask for?

If you couldn't get a copy of the guide, what else could you buy to find out about evening entertainments?

△ Perhaps you'll decide to do something a little more cultural – like these people.

Where are they and what are they doing?

For fans of black soul music, Dennis Brown is a must. If you decide to go and see him on the spur of the moment, how much will it cost you? ▽

Brighton has many different kinds of entertainment.

What sport would you be interested in if you decided to go here, and how much would it cost?

What would be the best time to arrive?

◁ The Buccaneer has other attractions for those who aren't keen on sport.

You'd probably be interested in two things if you went here. What would they be?

Your friend wants to come too, but doesn't know where it is. Can you tell her?

Is there any live music at the "Bop"?

Answers:

Have you got a copy of 'What's on and Where'?
The local newspaper.

They're at a theatre buying tickets.

It will cost £2.50.

You'd be interested in boxing.
It'd cost you 50p.
Probably just after 7.00 p.m.

Rock music and dancing.
It's opposite the Palace Pier, on the seafront.
Yes, there are two groups playing: Laughing Gass and I-Jax.

Your students might be interested to hear about other movements in 'Rock', e.g. Rock against Racism
        Rock against Sexism
        Rock against Nukes
        (nuclear power).

Aim	To teach some new idiomatic language relating to meeting people and making arrangements.
Background	The photos on this page provide a fairly representative sample of the kind of language students will encounter on similar posters throughout Britain.

Approach Students in pairs work on the questions in their books. Set a ten minute maximum time limit.

 Check answers with the class as a whole. (See opposite.)

Read the following story at normal speed:

The last time I was in Brighton, it cost me a fortune. I was *at a bit of a loose end* so I *got in touch with* an old friend, Jane. We had a long *natter* on the phone and she told me *to drop round* to her place — at *sevenish.* So I *set off* at 6.00 but got *side-tracked* when I *bumped into* another old *mate.* We called into a pub for *a quick one* which lasted two hours! When I got to the flat, Jane was really *put out.* She'd been *hanging about* for *well over* an hour. The only way I could *make it up to* her was to take her out for a *slap-up* meal. Mm — expensive that was — *set me back* 35 *quid* for *the pair of us. Pretty* stupid really — never was that crazy about her.

Ask: **How much did you understand?**
Go through it again, slowly, eliciting substitutions for the italicised words and phrases.

Students then work out mini-dialogues using the photos in their books and incorporating one or two of the new phrases, for example:

A   Why don't we go to the Buccaneer tonight?
B   O.K., but let's not hang about too long.
A   Fine. We can go to the pub after that — we'll probably bump into somebody we know there.

Extra

Railway Carriage
Write some of the new words and phrases on to cards. In pairs, the students enact a short scene in a railway carriage. They are strangers. Give each student one card with a new phrase written on it. Their aim is to start a conversation with the other person, during which they must use the phrase written on their card. As they get better at the game, put three or four phrases on the cards. This works best when the rest of the class knows what is written on each card.

PUBS

A	J
301	301
279	290
230	265
171	253
129	247
94	202

How to play darts

DARTS is Britain's most popular pub game. About 7 million people play every week. Professional darts players can earn up to £25,000 a year. It's an easy game to play – when you know the rules.

You have to begin and end the game with a double score, or else you can end on an inner bull, which scores 50. You start with 301 points. In this game, **A**'s first dart was a double 5 (total 10). Then she threw a 9 and a 3.

J started with a double 3 (total 6), then threw a 5. He missed the board with his third dart (he's not very good!).

A was the winner of the game. The darts on the board now show how she won. How did she do it?

Where would you see this sign? What's alcohol?

13

Comprehension questions:

How many people play darts every week?
What do you have to get before you can start the game?
How do you end the game?
What does 'professional' mean?

Practise numbers and prepositions by asking questions like these:

What's the number at the top of the dart board?
What's the number next to it on the left?
What numbers are next to 19?
What number is opposite 18?

Answer:

The girl won by throwing a **20** which brought her score down to **74**. Then she threw a double **12** which made her score **38**. Her last dart was a double **19**.

Extra questions:

What's another word for 'purchase'?
Can you buy beer in a pub if you're 17?
What if you're 18 but look younger?
How old must you be?
How old must you look?

Extra vocabulary:

football	footballer
swim	swimmer
run	runner
cricket	cricketer
golf	golfer
BUT tennis	tennis player

Aims	To give background information on a law which might affect students during their stay in Great Britain.
	To teach the use of 'must' and 'mustn't' for obligation.
	To teach basic vocabulary used in playing games.
	To show students how to play darts.
Background	Darts is the biggest participatory sport in Britain. Over 7 million people play every week.
	Children over 14 are allowed into pubs but they cannot drink alcohol or stand next to the bar. They must be accompanied by an adult.

Approach

Darts

Ask: **What's the name of this game?**
Do any of you play darts?
How many darts does each person have?

Basic vocabulary can be covered by asking:
What do we call a person who plays darts? (*player*)
                    a person who wins games? (*winner*)
                    a person who loses games? (*loser*)
(See 'Extra Vocabulary,' opposite.)

Students read text on 'Darts'. (See comprehension questions opposite.)

Under 18 Rule
Students read the sign and answer the two questions in their books. (Extra questions opposite.)

Extension of 'must' and 'mustn't', using the context of your school.

Ask: **Can you smoke in the classroom?** *No you can't.*
Give me a sentence with 'mustn't'
You mustn't smoke in the classroom.
What time does school start? *9.30*
Give me sentence with 'must'
We must come to school at 9.30.

Students practise 'must' and 'mustn't' with board prompts, for example:
noise/late/night
drive/left/English roads
stop/red traffic lights
if/under 18/go/pubs

Extra

Jumbled sentences to be worked out in pairs or groups. If in groups, give each person one word from the sentence to memorise. The group then has to organise itself physically into the correct word order.
Sentences:
a) drink pubs if you under you not alcohol must 18 in are
b) under drink the that alcohol 18 buy says or must law not people
Answers:
a) You must not drink alcohol in pubs if you are under 18.
b) The law says that people under 18 must not buy or drink alcohol.

PUBS
An interview
with a landlord

PUB seems a funny word. Why are pubs called pubs?

Yes, it is an odd word but really it's just short for 'public house', a place that has a special licence to sell drinks to people.

Why do most pubs have signs hanging outside them?

Because up to the beginning of this century, most people couldn't read, so a picture was the easiest way to show travellers where they could get a drink.

Ah, I see, but one thing I've noticed in Britain is that a lot of the pubs have the same name. I've seen at least three called The Red Lion. Why is this?

Well, many years ago, huge areas of Britain were owned by a small number of families, and clever inn-keepers named their pubs after these families who each had their own family symbol. For example, a Red Lion was the Gaunt family's symbol. The Tudors had a greyhound, that's why so many pubs all over the country have the same name.

Other pubs got their names from religious events, ways of travelling, sports, jobs, famous people, famous battles and so on...so you see – studying pub names is a really good way of learning a bit about our history.

I noticed when I came in that your pub's called a "free house". What does that mean?

Unfortunately it doesn't mean that the drinks are free! It's just that

most pubs are owned by big breweries like Watneys or Charringtons and so they only sell their own beer. But some landlords, like me, are lucky enough to own their own pubs and so they're free to sell any beer they like from any brewery.

Really....well this beer is lovely, it's very different from lager.

Yes, it's what we call real ale.

What's that?

Ah, that's a good question – and one that confuses a lot of tourists. Real ale's usually made by small local breweries so each type has a different taste. It's normally much stronger than the beer made by big breweries – when you're travelling round England you should try to taste some of the different types.

I will, I didn't realise there was so much choice. Do you have food here, I'm getting a bit hungry?

Yes, we've got sandwiches, pies, and a "Ploughman's" – do you know what that is?

I've no idea! What is it?

Well, it's bread, butter, cheese and pickled onions. Farmworkers used to have it for their lunch when they were working in the fields. Why don't you try one?

Mm — I will....

What are the names of these pubs?

Vocabulary:

optics (to give exact measures of spirits)
pump
barman/barmaid

Pub names:

The Five Bells
The Wobbly Wheel
The Spotted Dog

Pub Project

Using your knowledge of the local area, set up a project for the students to do in pairs (as long as they're over age!).
Points to cover could include the following:

Licensing hours
Differences between saloon and public bars
Kind of food served
Games played in pub
The most popular drink
Garden/children's room?

Decor
Music, e.g. live/juke box/tapes/piped musak
History/meaning of pub name
Free house/tied house/manager
Real ale sold?

Each pair should investigate a different pub and be ready to give a presentation of their discoveries to the rest of the class.

Aims	To give some information, through intensive reading practice, about an 'institution' which students are always curious about.
	To teach some useful 'pub' language.
Background	If your students are under 18, you might like to refer them to page 13 in the Student's Book. Here are some more facts you could give them during the lesson:
	Adults in the U.K. drink an average of more than 30 gallons of beer (136.5 litres) and less than 2 gallons of wine (9 litres) per year.
	About one third of the price of beer is tax. Tax on alcohol accounts for about 7% of total State revenue.
	10% of all spending on eating out is spent on meals and snacks in pubs.
	Great Britain is the third largest producer of beer in the world — the U.S.A. comes first and West Germany second.
	There are nearly 70,000 pubs in England and Wales; one in five is a free house.
	We have a greater variety of beer than anywhere else in the world. There are about 1,500 beers available here.

Approach Use general questions to introduce the subject.

Ask: **Do you like English pubs?**
Why?
What's the difference between English pubs and the bars in your country?
Which pub do you like best here?
Do you know the names of any other pubs around here?
(List some on the board)
Do you know why they have names like this?

 Students read the text,

 Suggested comprehension questions.

Imagine — it's 1880 and you're in a strange town. How do you know where to get a drink?
If you're the landlord of a free house, who do you buy your beer from?
What's special about 'real ale'?
What does the tourist decide to eat?

 Students look at the photos of pub signs and speculate on the names of the pubs. (Answers opposite.)

 Using the local pub names up on the board, ask the students how they think the pubs got their names.

Discussion on pub drinks.

Ask: **What do people drink in pubs?**

Teach combinations of drinks, paying special attention to pronunciation:
A pint o' bitter, half o' bitter.
Gin 'n tonic, ice 'n lemon, Scotch 'n soda.
Coke/orange juice/bitter lemon.
Teach: It's my round/cheers.
Mention British tradition of buying rounds of drinks in turn.

Extra See pub role play on Teacher's Book page 119.

A short history

Most foreigners find British pubs both fascinating and frustrating. Fascinating because they are unique to Great Britain and not at all like the bars you find in most other countries; and frustrating because of their peculiar opening and closing hours. In fact, much of the long history of pubs in Britain is to do with people who wanted to drink and others who wanted to stop them.

The development of pubs and the laws surrounding them is an interesting way of learning a little about our social history. Foreigners often think of tea as the British national drink, but compared to beer-drinking, tea-drinking is a very recent development.

Beer has been drunk in Britain since before the Roman invasion. The earliest breweries were part of

monasteries and as early as 695 AD the King of Kent was making laws in an attempt to stop priests from getting drunk.

The monasteries also provided food and beds for travellers. During the Middle Ages, it became so popular to make pilgrimages to famous religious shrines that inns had to be built because the monasteries could not look after the increasing numbers of pilgrims.

By the late 16th Century,

drunkenness was a real problem and laws were passed to restrict drinking-hours. In 1606, a law was passed which stated that the purpose of inns was to lodge "wayfaring people only". Travellers were allowed to buy drinks at times forbidden to local people. However, the ingenuity of the dedicated drinkers got round this problem and the result was that the locals would simply move on to the next town or village when they wanted to continue drinking after "time" in their own village!

In the 19th Century, cheap gin appeared in Britain. It was very popular among poor people. Drunkenness again increased and more laws were passed. The Temperance Society was formed to fight against "the demon drink". This group of dedicated teetotallers tried to persuade people to abstain from drinking by getting them to "sign the pledge". Today's equivalent of the Temperance Society is Alcoholics Anonymous, which

brings alcoholics together at weekly meetings and gives them a chance to help and support one another.

In spite of the various attempts to curb drinking, or stamp it out completely, pubs continue to provide a major part of British social

life. Their opening and closing hours are still restricted by law although there have been recommendations recently for big changes, including extending licensing hours and admitting children.

But nothing has happened yet. It may be that having lived with our strange laws for so long, we've decided that we don't really mind them after all, and that tourists will just have to learn to put up with them too!

53

Here are some opposites to try with your class. Read out a word from the left hand column and ask them to find a word in the text which has the opposite meaning. (Answers in brackets).

satisfying (frustrating)
normal (peculiar/strange)
common (unique)
demolished (built)
sobriety (drunkenness)
encourage (curb/stamp out)
minor (major)
well-known (anonymous)
restrict (extend)
ban (admit)

Aims		To give practice in summarising.
		To give students a short history of one of Britain's greatest institutions.
Background		A lot of the information and ideas at the earlier levels could be adapted for use with advanced students if your class is interested in the topic.

Approach

Students read the text while you put the following words and phrases on the board:
frustrating/unique/shrine/wayfaring people/ingenuity/teetotaller/curb or stamp out.
Ask students to *write* an explanation of each word.

Exchange and discuss explanations.

Suggested further comprehension questions.

Ask: **What's the name of a place which makes beer?**
Explain 'time' in paragraph 5.
Why are opening and closing times so restricted?
Explain 'demon drink' and 'sign the pledge.'

Ask students to write a short history of British pubs as an introduction to a 'Pub Guide For Foreigners' (like the Michelin or Shell ones). This should not exceed 150 words.
Point out that each paragraph has one main and several subsidiary facts. It is up to the students to select what *they* consider to be the most interesting facts for foreigners. The phrasing of their summaries should be their own, and nothing should be 'lifted' directly from the text.

Spend some time discussing *connectives* by writing the following on the board:

Although	Previously	In spite of
Because of	Eventually	
In order to	Subsequently	

Read out the following sentences and ask the students to connect them by using the words on the board.
1.   Dogs are useful. I don't like them. (although)
2.   I have a dog. It protects me. (in order to)
3.   I used to have a cat. Now I have a dog. (previously)
4.   Our house was broken into. We bought a dog. (subsequently)
5.   We thought about getting a dog for a long time. We bought one. (eventually)

Use one of their summaries as the introduction to the pub section of the student magazine.

Extra

Students compile a personal guide to the local pubs. See Teacher's Book page 54.

ANIMALS IN BRITAIN
Who cares?

The British are so mad about animals that they started a society on 16 June 1824 to prevent cruelty to them. Today the society is called the RSPCA and is a household name. The first royal supporter of the society was the then Duchess of Kent in 1835.

At present, there are over 240 inspectors who:
investigate complaints about cruelty to animals;
inspect livestock markets where animals are sold for food;
give talks to schoolchildren;
painlessly put down animals that are old or sick.
The RSPCA helps 170,000 sick animals a year.
It puts down nearly 200,000 animals.
It also finds new homes for 43,000 unwanted dogs and 29,000 cats.

What do you think RSPCA means?
What do you think the society was called before 1835? What does "put down" mean here?
Can you give any examples of household names in your own country? What's "livestock"?
What kind of advice do you think RSPCA inspectors give to schoolchildren?

Who owns what pets?

Fifty per cent of British families own a pet. There are 5.3 million dogs in 4.5 million households, 4.6 million cats in 3.3 million households and 2.5 million budgies in 1.7 million households.

Every week, most people spend about £1.55 on food for their dogs. Cat owners spend about 98p.

There are four main socio-economic groups in Britain. The AB group earns the most and the DE group earns the least. Between them are two other groups: C1 and C2.

23% of the population are AB
15% of the population are C1
33% of the population are C2
28% of the population are DE

Look at this graph.
What does it tell you about:
C2 families
budgies
C1 families and dogs
DE families?

14

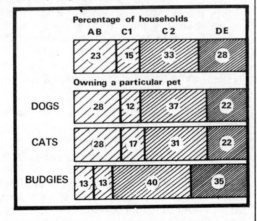

Percentage of households			
AB	C1	C2	DE
23	15	33	28

Owning a particular pet			
DOGS	28	12	37	22
CATS	28	17	31	22
BUDGIES	13	13	40	35

Here are some of the main things your students should mention when answering the graph questions:

C2 families: They are the largest socio-economic group. They own the most pets.

Budgies: Budgies aren't popular with AB & C1 families. 40% of C2 families own a budgie. 35% of DE families own a budgie.

C1 families and dogs: C1 families own the lowest number of dogs.

DE families: DE families own more pets than C1 families, but fewer than C2 families.

Here are some opposites to try with your class. Read out a word from the left hand column and ask them to find a word in the text which has the opposite meaning. (Answers in brackets.)

save	(spend)
allow	(prevent)
kindness	(cruelty)
lose	(find)
well	(sick)

Aims	To give intensive reading practice leading to logical working out of unknown vocabulary.
	To give practice in reading graphs.
	To give more practice in the pronunciation of numbers.
Background	Most foreigners believe that the British are completely mad when it comes to their attitudes towards animals. This page will probably reinforce that belief!

Approach

General questions:

Ask: How many of your host families have pets?
      What kind?
      How many of you have pets at home?
      Who's got a dog/cat?
      Who prefers dogs to cats? . . . and cats to dogs?
      Why do you like cats/dogs best?

Students read text on 'Who owns what pets?'

Ask: What's another word for 'household'?   *Family.*
      And for 50%   *Half.*
      Ask a question about dogs and households.
      Ask about cats.

      Board prompts if necessary: people/food/dogs/cats

Students look at graph and answer questions. (see opposite.)

Students read text on the R.S.P.C.A. and answer the comprehension questions — no help from you.

Check answers with whole class using the better students to explain the answers to the weaker ones where possible. (Answers opposite.)

Extra

Sequencing story

In this type of activity, each student is given a piece of paper with one or two sentences written on it. They are not allowed to show these pieces of paper to anyone else so they must reconstruct the story orally, by reading out their sentences to the rest of the class. Encourage them to sequence themselves physically. An element of competition can be introduced if you first divide the class in half. Edit or add to the story as necessary.

A similar technique can be used with short poems, in which case you can get the students to memorise their lines rather than reading them.

Here is one story you could use.

The Wilkins moved to a new house last year.
It was about 170 miles from their old one, and had a much smaller garden. The people who bought their old house agreed to keep the Wilkin's cat — Tiddles.
He was quite old and Mrs. Wilkins didn't think he'd be happy in the new house.
One evening, about a month after they'd moved in, they were watching television in the sitting room.
Mr. Wilkins thought he heard a strange noise in the garden.
He went outside and looked around.
He couldn't believe his eyes.
There, under a tree, very wet, very dirty and very thin, was Tiddles!

ANIMALS IN BRITAIN

Working animals

Richard commutes from Tunbridge Wells to Charing Cross every day. This difficult journey is made easier with the help of Raffles, his guide dog. Lorraine met him on the train....

Lorraine : What a lovely dog – how long have you had her?

Richard : ...Um...since July 1978.

L : Isn't it a bit unusual to have an alsation as a guide dog, aren't they usually labradors?

R : Yes, you're right. I did have a labrador before Raffles, but we were walking through London one day when an IRA bomb went off and it frightened her so much that she became unreliable.

L : Oh, I'm sorry to hear that. What happened to her?

R : She's fine, she's leading a life of luxury with a family in Rye.

L : What about Raffles, though, could you commute without her for instance?

R : Mm, yes...but much more slowly. On the other hand, people often overestimate what guide dogs can do.

L : Really – in what way?

R : Well, it's impossible to train them to cope with modern traffic, especially in London. The best she can do is to warn me of a dangerous situatioh.

L : How can she do that?

R : Simply by sitting down and refusing to move. I have to stand still and just hope that the driver misses me.

L : That must be a horrific experience....

R : Yes, it's not much fun!

L : Can I ask how much you paid for Raffles?

R : 50p.

L : What?

R : 50p...any blind person can buy a dog for 50p. Of course a lot of people pay more voluntarily, but the minimum price is 50p.

L : So public contributions on flag days for example, are really important...

R : Absolutely. The money, as you can see, is put to good use: these dogs have a very valuable working life.

General comprehension questions:

What kind of dog does Richard have?
What kind of dogs are usually used as guide dogs?
What happened to Richard's labrador?
How does Raffles help his journey?
How much do blind people have to pay for guide dogs?

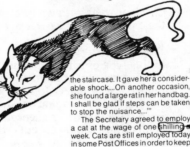

Here's a more unusual example of working animals. In December 1920 the Manager of a large Post Office in Bristol wrote to the Secretary of the Post Office in London: "...a night or two ago, a large rat dropped on the shoulder of one of the female cleaners as she was descending the staircase. It gave her a considerable shock....On another occasion, she found a large rat in her handbag. I shall be glad if steps can be taken to stop the nuisance...."

The Secretary agreed to employ a cat at the wage of one shilling ← 5p. a week. Cats are still employed today in some Post Offices in order to keep Britain's mail moving.

34

Potatoes Game

Buy as many potatoes as there are students in the class. Elicit/teach vocabulary to describe shape, texture and smell. Put the class into pairs, blindfold everybody. Give one person in each pair a potato. He/She describes it to the other who then touches it. Go around the class and mark each potato with the initials of the pair. Collect them and mix them up. Then hand them back to the pairs, who, still blindfold, feel them and pass them on until they think they have found their original potato.

Collect the potatoes. Remove blindfolds from one of each pair. Swap the potatoes around. The student without the blindfold should then describe the potato to his/her partner. Collect the potatoes. Re-distribute to the blindfold students who must try to identify 'their' potato purely from the verbal description of their partner.

| Aim | To point out and practise conversational gambits and 'lubricators' that we use habitually when talking to other people. |

Aim

To point out and practise conversational gambits and 'lubricators' that we use habitually when talking to other people.

Background

Students often sound less fluent than they really are because they don't get practice in the social 'lubricators' used in everyday English. Things like: leaning forward, raising an eyebrow, nodding your head, saying 'mm' at the appropriate moment, along with short responses like: 'Are you?', 'Is it?', 'Really!', make all the difference in conversations. This area can be actively taught but is often overlooked. We think that it makes ideal subject matter for a holiday course.

Approach

Vocabulary check. Using mime, if necessary, elicit/teach the following words: deaf/dumb/lame/blind/handicapped.

Discuss the problems of each particular handicap.

Ask: **If you're deaf, what problems do you have?**

Students will probably disagree quite strongly.

Pre-teach any essential vocabulary in the dialogue which you think your students might not know (See ringed words opposite.)

Students read the dialogue.

Ask general comprehension questions. (See opposite.)

Students pick out 'lubricating' sounds in the text: 'Um'/'Oh'/'Mm'. Discuss their uses, e.g. 'Um' just fills in a space while Richard tries to remember when he first got Raffles; 'Er' is a similar gap-filler. 'Oh' usually shows surprise of some kind; here it is immediately followed by an expression of sympathy. 'Mm' makes the following 'yes' far less definite.

Practise these sounds in context by asking quick questions and getting quick responses to statements.

Ask: **How long have you been here?** *(Er, since July 22nd)*
Do you like English food? *(Mm, some of it's O.K.)*
Did you know my dog got killed last week?
(Oh, I'm sorry to hear that.)

The intonation of 'Mm' is particularly important because if the intonation is wrong, the meaning of the sound changes completely. With a fast class, you could introduce a different meaning.

Ask: **Do you like champagne?** *(Mm, I love it.)*

Look at the following words and phrases with your students: in fact/for instance/for example/on the other hand/of course/well. These are bits of language we use naturally when we're explaining things to people. They give us an introduction to our sentences and give us time to think of what to say next.

Students read the text on 'The Post Office Cats'.

Students work out a dialogue between the Post Office Manager and the cleaner. He is questioning her to find our exactly what happened so that he can write a letter to the Post Office Secretary in London. They should build in short responses, 'lubricators,' and any other expressions which will make the dialogue sound as natural as possible. Ask some of the pairs to act out their dialogues to the rest of the class.

Extra

Potatoes Game. (See opposite.)

Put Animals into Politics!

All governments have allowed cruelty to animals.

Now is the time to stop it!

A large number of animal welfare and protection societies have come together in a single movement for the purpose of putting animals into politics. This unity is unique. We have six areas of immediate concern and we know that many thousands of people are looking to Parliament to introduce measures for the protection and welfare of animals in this country. OUR SIX AREAS OF CONCERN ARE: (Not in order of priority).

1 FACTORY FARMING
Where battery hens, calves and pigs are imprisoned in small cages, often for LIFE.

2 EXPERIMENTS ON LIVING ANIMALS
Where living animals are used for some highly questionable experiments and for testing cosmetics and other non-medical products which frequently cause acute pain and suffering.

3 TREATMENT OF HORSES
Where horses are treated cruelly by exposure and neglect. Where horses are transported hundreds of miles for slaughter to provide meat for the Continental table.

4 EXPORT OF LIVE FARM ANIMALS
Where farm animals suffer hardship and cruelty during transport both for overseas slaughter and further fattening.

5 DOGS IN THE COMMUNITY
Where dogs are left to stray, unwanted, and where the majority remain unlicensed, without a properly regulated system of centralised or local control.

6 BLOOD SPORTS
Where Public Opinion Polls indicate that the majority of people are in favour of banning "blood sports". That is, the hunting with hounds of otters, stags, hares and foxes and also live hare coursing.

The protection of animals against wanton and avoidable cruelty is of serious public concern. There can be no doubt of the importance of this subject. NOW is the time for POSITIVE ACTION. More and more voters are waiting to know where the political parties stand on this moral issue. Ask YOUR M.P. or Parliamentary candidates.

19 Queensferry Street, Edinburgh EH2 4PG, Telephone 031-225 2116   Chairman: Lord Houghton of Sowerby CH

General Election Co-ordinating Committee for Animal Protection

---

ANIMALS IN BRITAIN

Put animals into politics

1. What is the main concern of the *Put Animals into Politics* campaign?

2. Can you explain the words "stray" and "wanton"?

3. What meat comes from a calf imprisoned in a cage for its short life?

4. What makes this campaign unique?

5. What do most British people think about hunting?

We don't eat horsemeat in Britain and no-one seems to know the reason for this. Any ideas?

Does this page confirm or change any opinions you had about the British and animals?

Answers:

1. Unnecessary cruelty to animals.
2. Lost; unprovoked/careless.
3. Veal.
4. Different societies are campaigning together.
5. It should be banned.

---

muzzle

mane

snout   trotter   paw   nose   hind-legs   hoof/hooves

Here are some synonyms to try with your class. Read out a word from the left hand column and ask them to jot down a word from the text which means the same. (Answers in brackets.)

permit	(allow)
preservation	(protection)
killing	(slaughter)
prohibit	(ban)
preventable	(avoidable)

Aims	To provide background material before a visit to a zoo or wildlife park.
	To teach phrases used in arguments.
Background	A lot of summer courses organise visits to zoos and wildlife parks. These trips can lead to interesting discussions about the treatment of animals. This authentic newspaper advertisement was part of a campaign by various animal welfare groups which ran throughout the 1979 General Election. We think it will give your students a useful and different perspective on the British attitude to animals.
Approach	We expect this page to generate interest and discussion with little input from you.

 Ask the students to read the ad and answer the questions. (See opposite.)

 Do they think this is a worth-while cause or a waste of time? Pick up on any comments and produce an alternative point of view. Rally the class round different viewpoints and note the language the students use.

Either teach before the lesson, or highlight during it, the following phrases used in arguments:

Firstly/secondly/thirdly/finally,
In my opinion . . .
As far as I'm concerned . . .

I can see your point of view, but . . .
I can't possibly agree with that . . .
Yes, but don't you think . . . ?
Wouldn't it be better if . . . ?

I couldn't agree with you more . . .
Exactly . . .
That's just what I think . . .

Oh, come off it . . . you can't really mean/think that . . .
Are you seriously suggesting that . . . ?
That can't be true . . .

Some classes take to this kind of activity better than others, so it's important to have some alternatives in case the argument doesn't take off.

 You could teach some of the following idiomatic animal language: sheepish/catty/bitchy/to go to the dogs/to wolf down food/to let the cat out of the bag.

Also sayings such as: as cunning as a fox; as quiet as a mouse; as wise as an owl; as stubborn as a mule; as dead as a dodo.

Compare these ideas with the ways they are expressed in other languages. Get the students to translate and swap their own animal idioms.

Another amusing animal topic is how different languages express animal noises. Ask your students to compare their own with these: cock a doodle doo; quack quack; moo; woof woof/bow wow; miaow; baa.

| **Extra** | Practise the language used in arguments in a debate such as: 'Wildlife Parks are of no use to society and are cruel to animals,' or: 'A concern for animals breeds a concern for people'. |

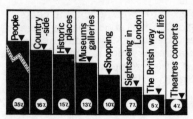

FOREIGN BRITAIN

Tourists

The British Tourist Authority asked some tourists "What did you enjoy most about Britain?" Here are their answers.

❝People think that the British are cold and unfriendly, but that isn't true. They're very friendly and they're always ready to help.❞
– *Antonella Rita from Italy.*

❝Here in Britain, the weather is really very mad. One day it's all windy and rainy, and the next – it's sunny and warm. I never know what clothes to wear.❞
– *Ahmed Kamali from Iran.*

❝I love the way you British speak – it sounds so correct.❞
– *Bernie Brown from USA*

Ask your students what we call people from:

Japan
Greece
Chile
Holland
Wales
Italy
France
Iran
etc.

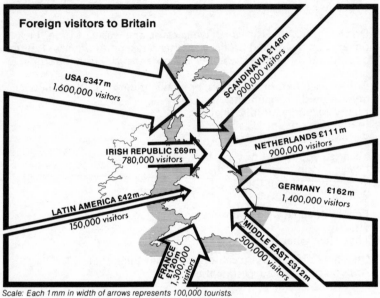

Scale: Each 1mm in width of arrows represents 100,000 tourists.

Look at this map.

Which nation brought the most money to Britain?
What does this map tell you about Scandinavian and Dutch visitors to Britain?

How much did each visitor spend, on average, while in Britain? Give an answer for each nationality.
Which nationality had the most money to spend? Which had the least?

15

Answers:

America.
The Scandinavians spent more than the Dutch.

USA . . . £216
Irish Republic . . . £88
Latin America . . . £280
France . . . £92
Middle East . . . £624
Germany . . . £115
Netherlands . . . £123
Scandinavia . . . £164

Most money . . . the Middle Easterners.
Least money . . . the Irish.

Aims	To practise extracting information from graphs and maps.
	To give the students an opportunity to express their own opinions on Britain and the British in a group writing exercise.
Background	Be prepared for quite a lot of criticism of Britain and the British. The weather is always a favourite moan and there are usually several things (like queueing and eating habits) which students think are stupid! It's worth keeping a note of these comments and coming back to them at the end of the course — their criticisms have usually mellowed considerably.
Approach	*The Graph*

Ask: **How many people enjoyed shopping most?**
            What did 35% of the tourists like most?
            Question — museums?
            Question — theatres and concerts?

Students ask and answer questions about the graph.

Students decide what *they* like most and least about Britain.

Pool all the results to make a class block graph similar to the one in the book.

Students read tourists' comments and write one single sentence each about their impressions of Britain or the British. After reading them out to each other in their groups, they organise the ideas into a logical paragraph. Either photocopy each paragraph so that each student can keep a copy, or transfer to a large sheet of paper and pin on the wall, or keep for the class magazine.

Students look at the map and answer the questions. (See opposite.) Further questions on the map with board prompts if necessary.

Say: **Question about France**
            Japan
            Germany
            £69 million.

Extras.

1. Students try to find out British opinions of *other* nationalities by asking their families.
2. Students interview other classes asking, 'What do you like most about Britain?' They then collate and transfer their results on to a large block graph which they design themselves.

FOREIGN BRITAIN

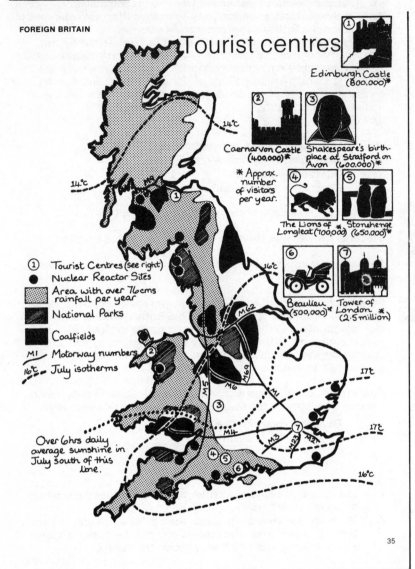

Tourist centres

Edinburgh Castle
(800,000)*

Caernarvon Castle
(400,000)*

Shakespeare's birth-
place at Stratford on
Avon (600,000)*

* Approx.
number
of visitors
per year.

The Lions of
Longleat (700,000)*

Stonehenge
(650,000)*

Beaulieu
(500,000)*

Tower of
London
(2.5 million)*

① Tourist Centres (see right)
● Nuclear Reactor Sites
Area with over 76cms
rainfall per year
National Parks
Coalfields
M1 Motorway numbers
16°C July isotherms

14°C

14°C

16°C

17°C

17°C

16°C

Over 6hrs daily
average sunshine in
July south of this
line.

35

The students should cover these points in their comments on the map:

The nuclear sites are all on the coast.
The major tourist attractions are mostly in southern England.
The coldest part of Britain is the north.
The wettest part is the west.
The warmest part is the south.
The driest part is the east.

All the motorways are near major industrial centres and coalfields.

An isotherm is a line which joins places of equal temperature.

Climate questions

Have the students seen the weather map on t.v. or in the paper?

Where does our weather usually come from?

Why does Britain have so much rain, and why does more fall in the west than the east?

If necessary, point out that moving wet air from the Atlantic rises over the mountains in the west. It cools and causes rain (condensation).

Answers to listening comprehension:

A = 6
B = 4
C = 1
D = 7
E = 3
F = 2
G = 5

Aims	To give intensive listening practice.
	To stimulate interest in the geography of Britain.
	To interpret a map and to make deductions from it.

Background All students will have studied geography at school. This can be exploited to stimulate language practice which they enjoy because they feel that they are having a rest from pure language learning.

Approach Students look at map.

Ask for comments about it. What can they say about the following:
— the position of the nuclear sites
— the position of the major tourist attractions
— the coldest and wettest part of Britain
— the warmest and driest part of Britain
— the number of motorways in the *centre* of the country.
(See opposite.)

Then read these four short listening comprehensions. The class should make notes and try to guess which tourist centre is being described, noting down their answers as you read. (Answers opposite.)

A.   This tourist centre in Southern England is Britain's National Motor Museum. It has over 200 old vehicles, including buses, cars, lorries, motor bikes and sports cars. It also has an enormous model railway, an audio-visual presentation about transport and a modern mono-rail which you can travel on. The centre is open all year round and admission is £1.50 for adults, and 75p for children under 13.

B.   This famous house is in southern England and was opened 25 years ago. It is a popular family attraction. There's an adventure playground, a huge maze where you can have fun getting lost, and lots of animals in the Safari Park, which is open every day except December 25th.

C.   Since 1861, every weekend at exactly 1.00 p.m., a gun is fired from this castle as a time check for the people who live in this capital city. The Scottish Crown Jewels are also kept here.

D.   Britain's most popular tourist centre contains the country's most valuable collection — the Queen's Crown Jewels. Many people have lost their heads in this 900 year old fort, which is always very crowded in summer.

Tell the students that you will give them three more centres later.

 Then ask them to speculate on the positions of the National Parks. Why do they think they are in the West of Britain? Is there any connection perhaps between this and the rainfall pattern? If so, what could it be? Give them a few minutes to think about this.

 Ask for ideas and guide the students towards thinking about the climate. (See questions opposite.)

 Then give the last three listening comprehensions.

E.   This house is now a museum and an information centre about Britain's most famous playwright, born in this town in 1564.

F.   The name of this castle means 'fort on the shore'. It was built between 1285 and 1322 in order to control the people in this part of Britain. The walls are two metres thick. Prince Charles was made the Price of Wales here in 1969.

G.   This ancient megalithic site was built in about 2000 B.C., and no-one really knows why. A fence has been built around it to protect the old stones from visitors — 650,000 a year. It is situated between Longleat, to the north-west, and Beaulieu Motor Museum, to the south-east.

Extra Students write a short paragraph summarising Britain's resources, climate and tourist centres.

FOREIGN BRITAIN

Ethnic minorities

Ethnic minorities often provoke emotional and uninformed opinions. In Britain there is a Commission for Racial Equality which tries to inform public opinion of the true facts rather than the myths. For example, many British people think that Pakistanis are the largest immigrant group but the bar-graph *(right)* shows that this is untrue. What **does** it show?

Here are some other myths that some people believe – and the facts.

MYTH: Immigration is making Britain an overcrowded island.
FACT: Since 1964 more people have left the UK each year than have entered. In 1976, 170,000 people came to live in Britain and 210,000 left, a net loss of 40,000. *(Office of Population and Census and Surveys.)*

Holland, Belgium and West Germany, all prosperous industrial countries, have more people per square mile than the UK. *(Pan World Atlas, 1973.)*

MYTH: Immigrants take British jobs.
FACT: During the 1950s and '60s, when there was a shortage of labour, like many industrialised countries we looked to other

countries to help us out. Eleven per cent of the total work-forces in West Germany and France, and 28 per cent of that in Switzerland, are migrants, compared with 7.5 per cent of workers in Britain.

MYTH: Blacks come here to sponge off the state.
FACT: Blacks, here, are a younger group than whites, so proportionately more blacks than whites are working and therefore paying income tax and national insurance. Of black men, 91 per cent are working compared with 77 per cent of white men.

Since there are proportionately fewer older people in the black community, they take less from the state than the white population.

MYTH: The black population of this country is many millions.
FACT: The latest estimate (mid-1976) of the size of the black population is 1¾ million – 3.3 per cent of the total population. In 1974 nearly 40 per cent of the black people had been born in Great Britain and therefore were not immigrants.

MYTH: Because they don't speak English they hold back our children at school.

Country	Number
IRELAND	709, 235
INDIA	321, 995
WEST INDIES	304, 070
AFRICA	164, 205
GERMANY	157, 680
PAKISTAN	139, 935
AMERICA	131, 540
POLAND	110, 925
CYPRUS	73, 295

FACT: Many children of immigrant parents were born here and English is their first language.

Most local education authorities make arrangements to teach English to non-English-speaking children in special classes with special teachers so that they do not impede the progress of the rest of the children.

There is no evidence that the proportion of black children in a class has any significant influence on the attainment of white pupils. *(Language Proficiency in the Multi-Racial Junior School: A Comparative Study, NFER, 1975; Race and Education across Cultures, Heinemann, 1975.)*

MYTH: Immigrants are running down British inner-city areas.
FACT: Urban decay has existed in this country since the Industrial Revolution. Bad housing conditions were here long before black immigrants. In the areas where 70 per cent of black people live, eight out of ten people are white. *(Census 1971.)*

55

Show your class this:
Poland, Polish, Pole.
Ireland, Irish, Irish man/woman.

Can they give the adjectives and nouns for the other countries on the graph?

Verb/noun changes:

Give your students the verbs in the left hand column, all of which are in the text. Ask them to supply the nouns that go with them. (Answers in brackets.) Point out any changes in stress and pronunciation.

inform	(information)
lose	(loss)
prosper	(prosperity)
compare	(comparison)
insure	(insurance)
progress	(progress)
attain	(attainment)
enter	(entrance)
exist	(existence)

Aims	To practise extracting information from a graph.
	To give practice in reading and saying numbers.
Background	For a long time now, immigration has been an emotional issue in Britain. Here, we try to present some of the facts as opposed to popular beliefs. The numbers practice is based on our own experience in teaching at this level. Fluent pronunciation of numbers seems to be a neglected area in the teaching of English abroad, so we suggest that you build in as much further practice as possible. Also, this is quite a gratifying area to work in because improvement is usually rapid, so the students really feel that they have achieved something.

Approach

Books closed. Ask students if they have any significant number of immigrants in their own countries.
Ask for a definition of 'immigrant'.

Ask: **Which do you think is the largest immigrant group in Britain? How do you think they affect life here?**

(List students' opinions for future reference)

Books open. Students look at graph and make sentences either beginning or ending with words which you put up on board, for example:

Start	*End*
The graph . . .	. . . the graph.
The largest . . .	. . . Cyprus.
The top three . . .	. . . 1971.

Books closed.

Ask: **What's the difference between a fact and a myth?**

The students should now check whether what they have already said was a fact or a myth by reading the text.
Check vocabulary: net loss/to help someone out/to sponge off/to hold back/to impede/to run down.

Oral test on pronunciation of numbers

Ask: **How many American immigrants live in Britain?** *131,540*
How many people left Britain in 1976? *210,000*
What percentage of black men work? *91%*
What percentage of the total population is black? *3.3%*
How many people came to live in Britain in 1976? *170,000*
Approximately how large was the black population in mid 1976? *1¾ million.*
When was there a labour shortage in Britain?
During the 50s and 60s.
What's the proportion of foreign workers in Switzerland? *28%*
In 1974, how many of the blacks living in Britain were immigrants? *60%*

Extra

Numbers dictation
(Students should write every figure in numbers.)
Here are some statistics about London: Total area 157,950 hectares. Numbers of residents: 8 million. Number of foreign visitors per year: 6.8 million. 49% of households have at least one car.
There are over 7.5 thousand miles of road and about 48,000 accidents a year. The average summer temperature is 16°C and the average winter temperature is 4°C. The first bus service opened on the 4th July, 1829. There are nearly 2,000 million passenger journeys on London Transport every year. In 1974, The London Fire Brigade received 87,307 telephone calls asking for help to put out fires.

Games, jokes and puzzles

Games, jokes and puzzles are an essential part of the language teacher's equipment.
They can provide:
- a five minute warm-up at the start of a lesson
- a further practice activity to reinforce specific language items
- general revision
- a change in pace and focus during a long lesson
- a 'filler' for the last ten minutes
- a way of creating a need, in the students, for specific pieces of language, which can be slipped in and practised without the students realising it.

When introducing new activities, make sure that all your students understand the instructions: begin by giving them, and then elicit them back from the class. Not all classes enjoy the same games — it's better to drop an unsuccessful one and replace it with another activity rather than bore the students to death. But try it with other classes before dropping it all together.

It's also worth remembering that higher level classes often enjoy 'silly' games, whereas lower levels can feel insulted by them. The selection of activities given here can be played in pairs, groups or singly. You could also give them as 'homework'.

Town Trail

This is a good out of class activity which can be
be done at all levels. The second week is a
good time to do this, when the students have
got to know the area better. Set up a quiz
which students do in pairs, leaving the school
at staggered intervals. Time their return —
the fastest pair are the winners.

Here are some examples of questions.

1. When do banks open and close?
2. What is the exchange rate for your
   foreign money? £1 =   ?
3. Can you name four daily newspapers
   printed in this country?
4. Where is the nearest chemist?
5. When does the chemist shop open and
   close on weekdays?
6. What is opposite the nearest police
   station?
7. What time is the last post on Saturdays?
8. Do traffic lights show:
   Red; red and amber; green; amber; red?
   or: Red; amber; green; red and amber; red?
9. Is the public library open on Wednesday
   afternoons?
10. Find the name of the nearest:
    sweetshop
    record shop
    stationer
    supermarket
    photographic shop.
11. What is the latest letter at the end of
    motor vehicle registration numbers?
12. How much does a gallon of four star
    petrol cost?
13. Which coins can you use in a telephone
    box?
14. Find out the phone numbers of:
    the tourist office
    the public library
    the police station
    the railway station.

The differences are:

lens on camera
headlights on bus
destination of bus
bus driver's shoe
handle on bag
fence behind bus driver
man's hair (over ear)
girl's hair (fringe)
tree branch
bus wheel

His parachute didn't open.

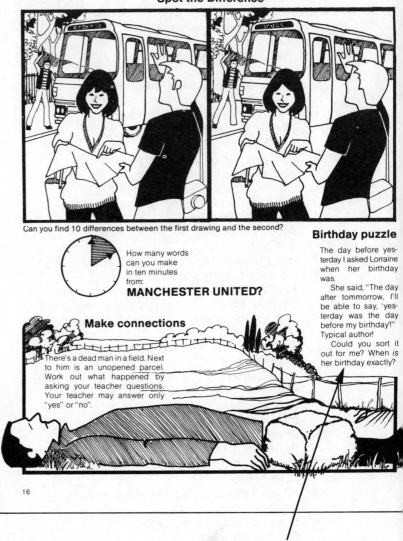

GAMES, JOKES AND PUZZLES

Spot the Difference

Can you find 10 differences between the first drawing and the second?

How many words can you make in ten minutes from:

MANCHESTER UNITED?

Make connections

There's a dead man in a field. Next to him is an unopened parcel. Work out what happened by asking your teacher questions. Your teacher may answer only "yes" or "no".

Birthday puzzle

The day before yesterday I asked Lorraine when her birthday was.

She said, "The day after tommorrow, I'll be able to say, 'yesterday was the day before my birthday'!" Typical author!

Could you sort it out for me? When *is* her birthday exactly?

16

Her birthday is today.

Do they know any others like this?

Birthday numbers

1. Multiply the number of your birthday month by 100. *E.g,* March is 300
2. Add the date of your birthday. *E.g,* If your birthday is 24 September 1964, you add 24.
3. Multiply this by 2 and then add 8.
4. Multiply this number by 5 and add 4.
5. Multiply this number by 10 and add 4 again.
6. Add your age to this result and then subtract 444.

The answer gives the month and date of your birthday, and your age! The first number or numbers of your answer is the month. The next number or numbers is the date of your birthday. The last two numbers are your age! Clever, isn't it?

Match box solution:

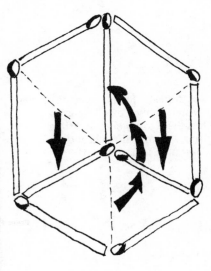

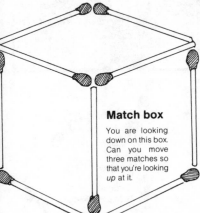

Match box

You are looking down on this box. Can you move three matches so that you're looking *up* at it.

Can you do this?

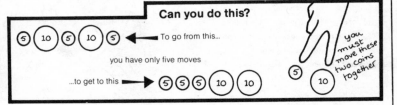

To go from this...

you have only five moves

...to get to this ➡

you must move these two coins together

17

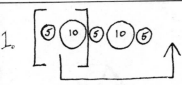

1.

4.

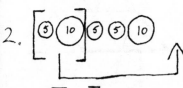

2.

5.

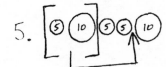

3.

73

The differences are:

people on escalator
reflection on glass
advertisement on far wall
buildings in left-hand poster
hair of girl on steps
right foot of man on right
shoulder-bag strap of girl in
foreground
the 'T' of LATE
hair of man in foreground

Ask students for examples of tongue
twisters in their own languages.
Get them to try ones in different
languages in multi-lingual classes.
Try doing some yourself!

GAMES, JOKES AND PUZZLES

Spot the Difference

Can you find 10 differences between the first drawing and the second?

Tongue-twisters

How many times can you say these without making a mistake?

She sells sea-shells by the sea-shore;

the shells that she sells are sea-shells, I'm sure.

Round and round the rugged rocks the ragged rascal ran.

Peter Piper picked a peck of pickled pepper,

a peck of pickled pepper Peter Piper picked.

If Peter Piper picked a peck of pickled pepper,

where's the peck of pickled pepper

Peter Piper picked?

The Leith Police dismisseth us.

36

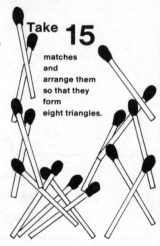

Take **15**

matches
and
arrange them
so that they
form
eight triangles.

* Don't forget the larger one.

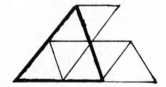

The Irish joke

People often tell jokes about other nationalities. In Britain there are thousands of jokes about the Irish. Here are some of them. What do they tell you about the Irish – from the British point of view? Do you have any jokes about the British?

There was an Irish pilot who was coming in to land at Heathrow Airport. The control tower asked for his "height and position". The pilot replied, "1 m 50 and sitting in the front."

What is written at the bottom of an Irish milk bottle?

What is there at the top of an Irish ladder? *

There was an Irishman working on a building site, who had an accident. His ear was cut off by a piece of machinery, so he went to see his boss and told him what had happened. His boss said that they should go and look for the ear because the doctors might be able to put it back on. After a few minutes the boss shouted, "Look, here it is!" The Irishman looked at it and said, "No, that isn't mine – mine had a pencil behind it."

"Why are Irish jokes so stupid?"
"Because otherwise the English wouldn't understand them!"

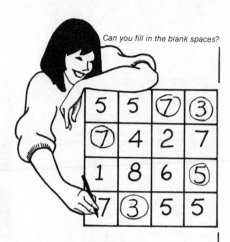

Can you fill in the blank spaces?

All the rows add up to 20.

* 'Open other end'.
  'Stop'.

Leslie is not Bob's brother, but Bob is Leslie's brother. What relation is Leslie to Bob?

Leslie is Bob's sister.

Can you arrange the words of this joke to fit the picture?

clocks...do...two... times...why... different...show... those...?

because...one...need... same...the...we'd... time...if...showed... they...only...!

37

Why do these clocks show two different times?
Because if they showed the same time, we'd only need one!

GAMES, JOKES AND PUZZLES

Crossword clues

ACROSS

1. Three points to view (3)
2. Mixed up ruse is certain (4)
4. Also, instrument without novice (3)
6. London to Cambridge for £50 in trip offer – is this a bargain? (3-3)
8. Usually has a limited following (2)
9. Preposition found in Oslo, Norway (2)
12. Property baron takes rent (8)
15. Meadow from mixed-up ale (3)
16. Night-club act (7)
18. Lucifer likes it like this (3)
19. Shorter than father (3)
21. Competent, but not totally capable (4)
23. Old-fashioned promise (6)
24. A short connection (2)

DOWN

1. Good man takes a turn to walk (6)
2. Gentle in lots of touches (4)
3. Unusual care is needed for this contest (4)
4. A spinning summit (3)
5. Frequently loses ten for genitive pronoun (2)
7. At home (2)

10. Mate without point is cooked (5)
12. Even a teetotaller would get a hangover from this (7)
13. A tidy whisky – without water (4)
14. Pat bad back (3)
17. Money given to treasury – it strains (5)
20. It's indiscreet to let the cat out of this (3)
22. To exist from beer with no queen (2)

The answer is GRAM.

DIA(----)MAR

Can you find a word which completes the first word and begins the second?

With 12 matches make 6 triangles;
with 12 matches make 14 triangles.

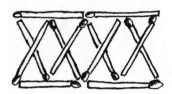

with 4 matches make 3 △s

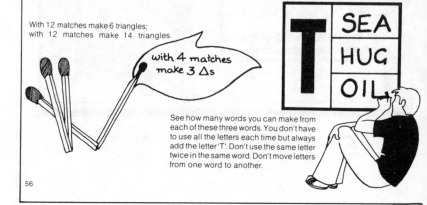

See how many words you can make from each of these three words. You don't have to use all the letters each time but always add the letter 'T'. Don't use the same letter twice in the same word. Don't move letters from one word to another.

56

3 triangles.

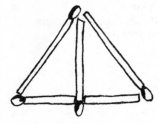

6 triangles.

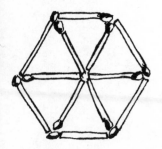

14 triangles.

Shown here is a highly diagrammatic map of mainland Europe. The countries are indicated by abbreviations, which should help you to identify them. (If not, there's always an atlas.)

Travelling only overland, can you visit all of the countries on the map once and only once?

If it is not possible to visit all of the countries as described above, what is the greatest number of countries that can be visited once and only once?

It's impossible to visit all the countries once and once only because of Denmark. The greatest number of countries that can be visited is 22.

Three dead men were found in a special room. There was one gun, one used bullet and one of the men was shot. How did the other two die and where were they?

They were trapped in a submarine. They drew lots to decide who would commit suicide with the gun. The other two suffocated.

— LET
— WIT
— LAY
— FIT

Which one word will complete these words?

The answer is OUT. (Teach meanings.)

Lost on the moon – problem sheet

You are in a space-crew originally scheduled to rendezvous with a mother-ship on the lighted surface of the moon. Mechanical difficulties, however, have forced your ship to crash-land at a spot some 200 miles from the rendezvous point.

The rough landing damaged much of the equipment aboard. Since survival depends on reaching the mother-ship, the most critical items available must be chosen for the 200-mile trip.

Below are listed the 15 items left intact after landing. Your task is to rank them in terms of their importance to your crew in its attempt to reach the rendezvous-point. Place the number 1 by the most important item, number 2 by the second-most important, and so on to number 15, the least important.

..... Box of matches
..... Food concentrate
..... 50 feet of nylon rope
..... Parachute silk
..... Portable heating unit
..... Two .45 caliber pistols
..... One case dehydrated milk
..... Two 100-pound tanks of oxygen
..... Stellar map (of the moon's constellation)
..... Life-raft
..... Magnetic compass
..... Five gallons of water
..... Signal flares
..... First-aid kit containing injection needles
..... Solar-powered receiver-transmitter

57

Answers to Lost on the Moon:

15. Box of matches — Little or no use on the moon.

4. Food concentrate — Supply daily food required.

6. 50 feet of nylon rope — Useful in tying injured, help in climbing.

8. Parachute silk — Shelter against sun's rays.

13. Portable heating unit — Useful only if part landed on dark side.

11. Two .45 calibre pistols — Self-propulsion devices could be made from them.

12. One case dehydrated milk — Food, mixed with water for drinking.

1. Two 100-pound tanks of oxygen — Fills respiration requirement.

3. Stellar map (of the moon's constellations) — One of the principal means of finding directions.

9. Life-raft — CO bottles for self-propulsion across chasm, etc.

14. Magnetic compass — Probably no magnetized poles; thus useless.

2. Five gallons of water — Replenishes loss by sweating etc.

10. Signal flares — Distress call within line of sight.

7. First-aid kit containing injection needles — Oral pills or injection medicine valuable.

5. Solar-powered receiver-transmitter — Distress signal transmitter, possible communication with mother ship.

77

A TASTE OF BRITAIN

A menu

VAT
REG. NO
190·3250·85

PRICES
INC
VAT

To Begin

MACKEREL MOUSSE
A rich, creamy paté of mackerel, hardboiled eggs and gherkins **75p**

SOUP OF THE DAY specially prepared by the Sussex Kitchen **40p**

THE CREAMY CRAB COCKTAIL A Pelham Speciality **85p**

A COCKTAIL of mixed orange and grapefruit **60p**

HOME MADE PATÉ OF THE HOUSE **75p**

PRAWN COCKTAIL **75p**

Continuing

CASSEROLE OF CHICKEN
Cooked in a cauldron with red wine, olives and mushrooms and including a selection of vegetables **£2.20**

THE PELHAM PIE Steak and kidney, homemade, served in a rich, dark sauce and including vegetables **£2.10p**

SUSSEX FISH DISHES
Scampi & goujons of sole, deep fried golden. Served with petit pois, French fried potatoes, tartare sauce **£2.60**

PRIME FILLET STEAK grilled to your choice and served with a selection of vegetables **£3.85**

TOSSED GREEN SALAD **40p**

ESCALOPE OF VEAL
Fried in butter, herbs & garlic served with a selection of vegetables **£2.60**

SPECIAL DISH tonight:– see table card

To follow

PELHAM POT O'CHOCOLATE **65p**

HOMEMADE MERINGUE and fresh cream **70p**

A selection of ICE CREAM or SORBETS **55p**

SYLLABUB **70p**

VANILLA ICE CREAM with chocolate or butterscotch sauce **65p**

Selection from the CHEESE BOARD with French bread, biscuits and butter **65p**

Cona Coffee 25p black or with cream. Cover charge to include bread & butter 15p
Service NOT included, excepting parties of 5 or more when 10% may be added

WINE LIST OVERLEAF

What's the name of this restaurant?
Can you think of other words for "to begin" "to continue", "to follow"?
How many home-made things can you see here?

What are they? Who made them?
The name "French fried potatoes" is American.
What do we usually call these potatoes in England?
Where's the wine list?

18

Practise pronouncing prices.

Answers:

The Pelham.
Starters, Main course, Pudding/
Dessert.
Soup of the day, paté, steak and
kidney pie, chocolate pudding,
crab cocktail, meringue and cream.
Home made things are made by
the people who own, or work for,
The Pelham.
Chips.
On the other side of the menu.

Aims	To introduce general 'menu' and food vocabulary.
	To teach some of the simple language needed to order food in cafés and restaurants.
Background	If the students have a particular café or restaurant they use regulary, try to get some menus and work from them. Make sure your students know that you don't snap your fingers or clap your hands at waiters or waitresses in Britain!
	'I'd like', which appears on Teacher's Book page 17, could be revised here.

Approach

Ask: **When you go into a café or restaurant, what do you read before you order your food?**
What do we call the person who brings the food?
Which cafés do you go to here?
What do you usually eat (list on board)
How much does it cost?
What do you say when you ask for your food?

Practise: 'Could I have . . . please,' and '(I think) I'll have . . . please', using the list on the board.
Note: *some* soup/potatoes/toast etc.
a salad/steak/glass of wine etc.

Ask: **You want the menu — what do you say to the waiter?**
Could I have the menu please?
When he comes to take your order, what does *he* **say?**
What would you like?
You want something that isn't on the menu — what do you say to the waiter?
Have you got . . .?

Set up a dialogue across the class between waiter and customer, for example:

Waiter	What would you like?
Customer	Could I have . . .? Oh, and have you got . . . ?
Waiter	No, I'm sorry, we haven't.
Customer	Okay, I'll have . . . then.

Students read text and answer questions in book. Go through answers (opposite) pointing out V.A.T. and service charge.

Extra

The students write short reviews of cafés/pubs/restaurants they use. Discuss the headings they could work with:
prices/location/quality of food/size of portions/hygiene/cleanliness/friendliness of staff.
These can be pinned up for the students in other classes to read, or be used in the student magazine.

A TASTE OF BRITAIN

Descriptions and opinions

sour "off" soggy gooey creamy sickly mushy stringy rich sticky sharp crunchy bitter chewy

Can you use these words to describe the foods below?

a lemon   last week's milk   a cucumber   peanuts undercooked cake   toffees   a bar of milk chocolate too many bars of milk chocolate!   old green beans very strong coffee   cream-filled meringues overcooked boiled potatoes

Students' opinions about English food

"English people don't cook with love...."

"You can't make coffee in England, it tastes of nothing and it's sour."

"I don't like English breakfasts because I don't like hot food in the morning."

"English people eat only for living, not for enjoying"

"I think English food is quite nice. I'm surprised because all my friends say that it's awful."

What's your opinion?

Why not try making these crunchy toffee apples?

Toffee apples don't keep well and you should eat them on the same day as you make them. You will need:

6 ice cream sticks, 6 crisp eating apples (*Granny Smiths are best*), 150gms of sugar, 75ml water, 1 teaspoon lemon juice, a heavy saucepan and a large piece of foil rubbed with a little oil.

What to do. We've mixed up these instructions. Can you put them in the right order?

Then turn up the heat and boil the mixture for a couple of minutes.
Pull out the stems and push the sticks into them.
If the toffee in the pan gets too thick, turn on the heat for a short time.
Wash and dry the apples.
Wait for the sugar to dissolve – don't stir.
Stand each apple on its end on the foil.
When it becomes a golden colour, turn off the heat.
Put the sugar, lemon and water into the saucepan over a LOW heat.
Quickly dip each apple into the toffee, one at a time.
Put in a cool place and leave them for a couple of hours – if you can!
Hold the apple over the pan until the toffee gets hard.

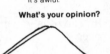

38

Either: get the students to sequence this in pairs.

Or: rewrite the sentences on slips of paper and do this as a physical sequencing exercise. See instructions on Teacher's Book page 59.

An acceptable order is:

Wash and dry the apples.
Pull out the stems and push the sticks into them.
Put the sugar, lemon and water into the saucepan over a LOW heat.
Wait for the sugar to dissolve — don't stir.
Then turn up the heat and boil the mixture for a couple of minutes.
When it becomes a golden colour, turn off the heat.
Quickly dip each apple into the toffee, one at a time.
Hold the apple over the pan until the toffee gets hard.
Stand each apple on its end on the foil.
Put in a cool place and leave them for a couple of hours — if you can!
If the toffee in the pan gets too thick — turn on the heat for a short time.

Answers to food descriptions:

Lemon . . . sharp/bitter/sour
Last week's milk . . . sour/'off'
Cucumber . . . crunchy
Undercooked cake . . . soggy/gooey
Toffees . . . chewy
Bar of milk chocolate . . . creamy
Too many bars of milk chocolate . . . sickly
Old green beans . . . stringy
Very strong coffee . . . bitter
Cream filled meringues . . . gooey/sickly
Overcooked boiled potatoes . . . mushy

Aims	To teach some idiomatic adjectives used in describing food.
	To practise the language used to ask for and give opinions.
Background	Holiday courses give teachers a great opportunity to exploit idiomatic vocabulary areas. Students enjoy learning idioms, so we hope that this page will provide a starting point for further less formal vocabulary work.

Approach Introduce the idea of describing taste sensations by taking the following items into class: a packet of crisps, a bar of chocolate, some apples, some lemons. Divide the class into four groups. Give one item of food to each group. Ask them to taste the food then write down some adjectives which describe the taste. After each tasting, the groups should change to another item. Once each group has tasted everything, write the items on the board and build up lists under each one. Feed in and practise new adjectives when their own are inadequate or inaccurate. Aim to end up with something like this:

Crisps	Chocolate	Apples	Lemons
salty	creamy	hard	sour
crunchy	smooth	sweet	sharp
crispy	sweet	crunchy	bitter

Introduce qualifiers. *very* sweet, *too* sour, *really* creamy, *slightly* sweet, *fairly* salty, *quite* sweet.

 Students look at the first section of the text. By process of elimination, using the adjectives they already know, they should be able to work out at least some of the descriptive meanings of the unknown adjectives.

 Compare hypotheses, give correct interpretations where necessary. (Answers opposite.)

Ask them to think of other food items which could be described by these adjectives.

Asking for and giving opinions

 Students read the text.

 Revise/teach the ways in which we ask for other people's opinions:
What do you think about/of . . .?
What's your opinion about . . ./of. . .?
How do you feel about . . .?
Do you think that . . .?
Point out that prepositions are normally followed by the 'ing' form of the verb, e.g. 'What do you think about *eating* bacon and eggs for breakfast?'
Revise/teach the ways in which we introduce opinions:
I think that . . ./I don't think that . . .
I feel that . . ./I don't feel that . . .
I'm sure that . . ./I'm not sure that . . .
In my opinion . . .

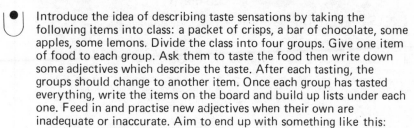 Across the class, students ask each other for their opinions of English food.

Extra *Sweet or biscuit survey*
The students should aim to find the best quality and best value for money from a sample of well-known sweets or biscuits. Their findings should be based on. flavour; how long the flavour lasts; attractiveness.
Pass a sample of sweets or biscuits around the class for tasting, timing and comments on appearance. Students work out and give reasons for: the best buy; the worst buy; the biggest disappointment.

A TASTE OF BRITAIN
Fast food

In the past ten years or so, America's most popular export to Britain has been THE HAMBURGER. One very well-known American company which has restaurants all over the world even has its own "university". Here, if you fancy becoming an expert in the subject, you can take a ten-day course leading to the "degree" Batchelor of Hamburgerology. If you get really interested in the subject, you can even go on to do your Master's degree – but that takes longer!

Hamburgers are, of course, fast food: they don't take long to cook and they take even less time to eat. The ideology of fast-food restaurants centres on the time it takes to get the customer in and out of the building.

Next time you're in one of them, look around. You'll notice that they aren't usually very comfortable (they don't want to encourage you to hang around for too long). And they're normally decorated in bright, garish colours because pyschological tests are supposed to show that this makes people hungrier. The chips – oops, sorry, we mean French Fries – have a rather peculiar texture. This is because they're made from granules of dried potato which are put into a machine, mixed with water, then squeezed out of a square tube so that they resemble real French Fries.

Thirsty? Why not try a milk-style shake. Again, don't expect to get real milk...why bother with the real thing when you can buy milk powder which doesn't go off, and when added to water makes almost the real thing?

Keen students of English should read the menus in these places. If you think you could do with improving your vocabulary, especially adjectives, study them with care.

Eat, drink and be merry

A lot of countries now have very strict laws about drinking and driving. In Britain, for example, the legal limit for alcohol in the bloodstream when driving is 80mg. of alcohol per 100ml. of blood. In other words, if you drink more than about two pints of beer, you shouldn't be driving.

Of course, the effect of the same amount of alcohol on people of different ages and weights varies quite a lot. And if you drink on an empty stomach, the effect will be much quicker because the alcohol is more easily absorbed into the bloodstream.

If you are stopped by the police and suspected of being drunk, they will breathalyse you. This involves blowing into a bag containing clear crystals. If they turn green this shows, roughly, that you could be over the limit and you will be asked to go to the police station for a further test.

If this proves positive, you will be prosecuted. On conviction, disqualification from driving for a year is normally automatic, together with a fine of up to £400 and/or imprisonment for up to two years.

The two-pints-of-beer limit is well-known, but people often forget the alcoholic content of other drinks. Foreign visitors are often confused by our eccentric way of measuring drinks. What do you think is the alcoholic content of the drinks at the top of the page compared with a pint of beer? Left to right, they are: a large glass of scotch, two glasses of sherry, two glasses of wine and two thirds of a pint of cider.

They're all the same.

Knickerbocker Glory   60p
A long luscious combination of strawberries, fruit cocktail and ice cream – the summit sprinkled with chocolate vermicelli.

Banana Long Boat   60p
A whole banana, split lengthwise, with fruit cocktail and a jumbo-size portion of ice cream topped with chocolate vermicelli.

58

Fun food idioms:

butterfingers
cheesed-off
to play gooseberry
to blow a raspberry
a load of tripe

Ask the students to translate and explain some of the food idioms in their own languages.

Students are often interested in the differences between American and British English. Here are some related to food:

British	American
ketchup	catsup
chips	french fries
biscuit	cookie
sweets	candy
pudding	dessert
to grill	to broil
crisps	chips
packed lunch	sack lunch
transport cafe	greasy spoon

Aims	To introduce some unusual food vocabulary.
	To show how alliteration, metaphor and onomatopoeia are used to achieve certain stylistic effects.
	To give information on drinking and driving laws in Britain.
Background	Students seem to enjoy eating in American-style fast-food outlets, which are becoming increasingly popular in Europe and Japan. We thought you might like to capitalise on the language that's being imported with the food.

Approach   Books closed.

Draw  on the board.

Ask: **What's this? Describe it.**
(Insist on precise language.)
How do you like the meat cooked? *Rare, medium, well done.*
What do you like with it?
Fried/raw onions, tomato ketchup, pickles, chips/french fries.

Books open. Students read the text.

Explore the style with some general questions.

Ask: **Why are 'university' and 'degree' in inverted commas?**
What does the writer think about fast food generally and psychological tests in particular?
Would you say that the style is formal or informal?
Which particular words or phrases support your view?

Check vocabulary: to centre on/garish colours/granules/squeezed out of a square tube/resemble/to go off.

Students look at the meanings and comment on use of the following words and phrases on the menu: long luscious/summit sprinkled/ jumbo size/topped.

Discuss the style and effect of the following features.
Alliteration
The use of words, close together, which begin with the same first letter, as in 'long luscious'.
Further examples: 'peanuts packed with power,' and 'sun-soaked satsumas'.
Metaphor
The use of words which are not usually applicable to the context.
'Summit' usually means the top of a mountain, so here it implies that the ice cream is very large.
Further examples: 'golden layers of cheese,' 'curry served on a bed of rice', 'coated with rich chocolate sauce'.
Onomatopoeia
A word which sounds like its meaning e.g. 'smooth'.
Further examples: *'sizzling* sausages', *'crunchy* biscuits', 'pork *crackling.*

Do students know or can they guess, the meaning of the following?
tick tock,   boom,   splash,   squelch,   whizz,   twitter,   squirt,
clap,   crunch.

Eat, Drink and be Merry
Divide the class into two teams and get them to ask and answer questions on this text. See notes on Teacher's Book page 41.

Extra   (See opposite.)

INTO THE EIGHTIES
Computers

The newest industry in Britain is micro-electronics and computers. It is growing very quickly. 25 years ago, most computers weighed about 3 tonnes and cost about £100,000. Today the same computer weighs less than a kilo and costs £150.

This is all because of the micro-processor which carries electronic messages on a thin piece of silicon. You can see how small it is in the photo.

People often think that computers are clever but all they know is the difference between 1 and 0. It is

the computer programmer who uses this fact to make the computer do different jobs. Today a computer can do 100 million calculations in ONE SECOND. We already use microprocessors in our everyday lives *(below)*.

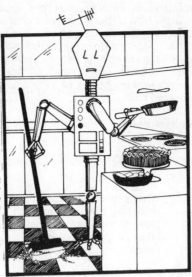

display   key

But computers are doing other things....

Did you know that:
In America, you can buy a robot for £2000. It cleans floors, mows lawns and does simple cooking;

in the American Prairies there are driverless tractors to cut the wheat;

in a town called Tama, near Tokyo, they have TV sets that print newspapers in your own home;

In Britain, a computer called Muppet can translate 50 words from English to French and vice versa.

19

This could be a good place to teach some mathematical symbols:

+	add/plus
—	subtract/minus
×	multiply
÷	divide
√	square root
=	equals
%	per cent

All these symbols are found on most calculators

Vocabulary used in operating machines:

Switch on/off a t.v. set.
Turn up/turn down the volume.
Press the button to change channels.

Pull/push doors.
Insert coins into slots.

Aims	To give practice in intensive reading and listening, leading to simple note taking.
	To give more practice in forming questions.
Background	You may find that the students know quite a lot about computers in their own countries, so give them the opportunity to talk freely.
	Make a note of mistakes *and* good points, and deal with these later.

Approach

Ask: **What do you know about computers?**

Note students' responses on the board.
Students make complete sentences from the notes combining two ideas where possible.
For example, *notes on board*: cheap/useful/quick/small; *sentence*: 'Today, computers are cheap and work very quickly'.

Ask: **Which words disappear when we make notes?**

Ellicit/teach definitions of conjunctions, prepositions, nouns, adjectives, verbs, adverbs. Ask students for examples.

Students read the first two paragraphs in their books and put them into note form.

Write up one or two of their suggestions on the board.

Students read third paragraph, make their own notes and exchange them. Then they put each other's notes back into sentences without referring back to the text.

Students read back first two paragraphs from notes on board.

Extra

Dictation
Read through completely then read each sentence twice at normal speed.

Relax — the computers are coming. Sit back — put your feet up and let them do the work for you. Did you know that some hospitals in London use computers instead of doctors? If you're ill, you have an interview with a television which asks you questions about your illness. All you do is answer Yes or No.

And in Germany and France, they use robots with metal arms to wave flags and warn motorists about roadworks. The French robot smiles — the German one doesn't.

But computers will soon teach you English. There won't be any more books and there will be very few teachers. Instead you'll watch television and listen to tapes, and you will practise your grammar again again and again and again and again and again . . .

Get each student to write up part of the dictation on the board. They can then correct each other collectively.

INTO THE EIGHTIES

What is happening here?

Answer:

The man is saving fuel and money, and making himself healthier, by driving only part of the way to his destination. He then parks the car, takes his foldaway bike out of the boot and cycles the rest of the way.

The National Centre for Alternative Technology

The people at Britain's National Centre of Alternative Technology in Wales are trying to find ways of using less energy. They also believe that we should make more use of natural resources like the sun, wind and water.

They grow their own food without using chemicals and keep animals to provide milk, meat and manure. The centre began in 1974 and about 80,000 people visit it every year.

Some people think that nuclear power is the answer to our energy problems. Others, including those at the NCAT believe that we must learn to use less energy and develop safer alternatives to nuclear power. Research into alternative technology is growing as the energy crisis gets worse.

CAR +
speed
comfort
space

BICYCLE +
economical
quiet and
clean
healthy

CAR —
petrol
traffic jams
maintenance

BICYCLE —
weather
long journeys
luggage

Can you make sentences using these ideas and then think of more advantages and disadvantages?

39

e.g. a bicycle is more economical than a car.
a car is more comfortable than a bike, especially when it's raining.

Useful car and bike vocabulary:

Car: boot/roof/windscreen/ windscreen wipers/tyres/ puncture/steering wheel/ bonnet/exhaust.

Bike: saddle/handlebars/brakes/ wheel/spokes/pump/bell.

Aims	To give some information about energy consumption and alternative technology.
	To practise and consolidate language used in arguments.
Background	Most students have strong ideas concerning the energy situation today. You can exploit these to practise the language of arguments. You may find it useful to have some additional facts up your sleeve:

The annual cost, at January 1980, for heating a 3 bedroomed semi-detached house in Britain:

£200	gas;	£330	off-peak electricity;
£230	coal;	£360	oil.

An average family saloon car uses more oxygen in a 600 mile (960 km.) journey than a human does in a lifetime.

On an average transatlantic flight with the plane half full, a passenger will 'use' about 4 times his/her own weight in fuel.

The amount of solar energy which falls on 30 sq. kms of earth each year is equal to the whole amount of energy Britain uses in a year.

Approach 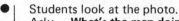 Students look at the photo.

Ask: **What's the man doing? And why?** (Answer opposite.)

Students look at cartoon and make sentences about advantages and disadvantages. (See opposite.)

Students read the text while you put the following phrases on the board:

1. Alright, but don't you think . . .?
Fair enough, but what about . . .?

2. Personally, I think that . . .
If you ask me, I think . . .
In my opinion . . .
As far as I'm concerned . . .

3. I hate to disagree but . . .
On the other hand . . .
(I'm sorry, but I can't go along with you on that . . .)

4. That's a good point . . .
That's exactly what I think . . .
(I couldn't agree with you more)

Ask: **What happens at the NCAT?**
Do the students have anything like this in their own countries?

Point out that the language on the board is used when people are having a discussion or an argument. Help them to work out when each would be used.

1. In challenging an argument.
2. In stating an argument.
3. In disagreeing with an argument.
4. In agreeing with an argument.

 Students work on mini-dialogues (two or four lines) which illustrate the points just discussed, for example:

1. *A* In my opinion, bikes are much healthier than cars.
B Fair enough, but what about long journeys?
2. *A* As far as I'm concerned, bikes are a waste of time.
B O.K., but on the other hand, cars are a waste of energy.
3. *A* Cars are essential for people with families who live in the country.
B That's a good point!

Depending on time, you could either go straight into the role play on Teacher's Book page 118, or leave the subject for a day and then return to the role play, in which the above language should be used.

INTO THE EIGHTIES
A computer flowchart

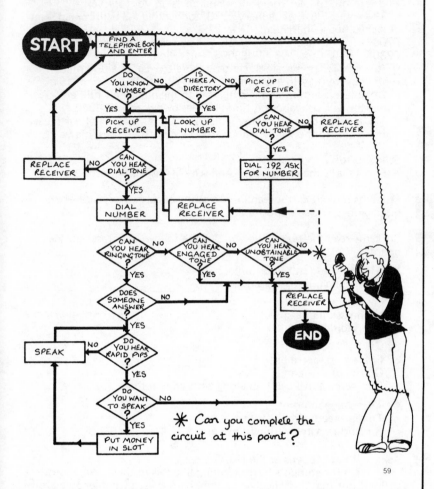

START

FIND A TELEPHONE BOX AND ENTER

DO YOU KNOW NUMBER? — NO → IS THERE A DIRECTORY? — NO → PICK UP RECEIVER

YES

PICK UP RECEIVER

LOOK UP NUMBER

CAN YOU HEAR DIAL TONE? — NO → REPLACE RECEIVER

YES

DIAL 192 ASK FOR NUMBER

REPLACE RECEIVER — NO

CAN YOU HEAR DIAL TONE? — NO → REPLACE RECEIVER

YES

DIAL NUMBER

REPLACE RECEIVER

CAN YOU HEAR RINGING TONE? — NO → CAN YOU HEAR ENGAGED TONE? — NO → CAN YOU HEAR UNOBTAINABLE TONE? — NO

YES   YES   YES

DOES SOMEONE ANSWER? — NO

YES

REPLACE RECEIVER

END

DO YOU HEAR RAPID PIPS? — NO → SPEAK

YES

DO YOU WANT TO SPEAK? — NO

YES

PUT MONEY IN SLOT

✳ Can you complete the circuit at this point?

59

Answer:

*Very often, your call doesn't 'go through'. In this case, you have to replace the receiver and start again. Therefore, there should be a line from 'No' to 'Replace Receiver'.

Aims	To revise telephone vocabulary.
	To practise using *precise* language for description and instructions.
Background	We have included this page because we feel that the 'Olde Worlde' view of Britain, which is so often presented to foreign tourists, needs to be balanced by a more up-to-date image. Although the page could be used on its own, it could also provide a starting point for further discussion of the latest developments in computer technology. We have kept to the basic principles involved in devising a flow chart because of the speed at which the industry is developing. Some of your students may have quite a lot to say about this subject because computer technology is now taught in many schools abroad. A flow chart is a pictorial breakdown of a problem into its logical steps, each of which must be as simple as possible in order for the computer to understand the orders that will eventually be programmed in.

Approach

Students work through the flowchart. One student acts as the computer, asking questions and giving instructions, while the other, who doesn't look at the book, answers the questions. They should run through the chart about four times, changing roles each time. In this way, they ought to get a good idea of how the chart works.

While the students are working on this, write some questions on the board:

What kind of questions is a computer able to ask?

What's the difference between square-enclosed and diamond-enclosed text?

How many 'loops' are there in the chart?

What has probably happened at *? (See opposite.)

What does the chart tell you about computers?

In groups, students work out a flow chart for crossing the road. Here's what it should look like:

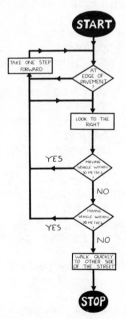

Extra

We've included another flowchart for your entertainment, on Teacher's Book page 121, which you might like to share with the students!

Out and about in London

Nearly all students will want to visit London during their stay in Britain. A day visit is always exhausting and can turn out to be little more than a coach tour and endless queueing. However a bit of forward planning can help you and your students to get more out of the day. The three double pages on London are included in order to give you some ideas, and an opportunity to do some class preparation before the visit.

Here are a few points to bear in mind before you start:

- Visiting London in the summer is hard work, so don't attempt to do too much in one day.
- Avoid walking around in a large group. Better to split into smaller groups, based on common interests, because these are easier to control and harder to lose.
- You need as many teachers and helpers as possible.
- Plan as much of the trip as possible in advance, *with your students.*
- The best compromise is a coach tour of the sights in the morning, followed by particular trips in the afternoon.
- Divide the students into smaller groups for the afternoon.
  Suggest activities like: A visit to a gallery or museum.
  St. Catherine's Dock and The Tower.
  A trip to Greenwich.
  A walk down Whitehall, Downing St. and around Westminster Abbey.
  A walk around Piccadilly, Trafalgar Square and Covent Garden.
- Arrange a rendezvous, making sure that all your students can ask for a *specific* place if they get lost.
- Think about lunch. If you have packed lunches and a coach — use it. If not, use a park.
- All the students will want to do some shopping — so remember to allow about an hour for this.

Elementary

Before starting the students on the quiz, teach or revise expressions such as:

I think the answer is . . .
No, I don't agree. I think it's . . . because . . .
This must be the right answer . . .
It can't be the right answer . . .
What do you think?

Students work through the quiz — allow 30 minutes maximum.
(Answers on Teacher's Book pages 92-93.)

General knowledge quiz should be done as a listening comprehension, with the students working in pairs.

1. What's the name of the Queen's house?
2. Give the names of two London railway stations.
3. Where are the Crown Jewels?
4. Where can you find Admiral Nelson?
5. What's 'Harrods'?
6. Give the names of two London churches.
7. How do you spell the name of the river that runs through the centre of London?
8. Which is London's most famous clock?
9. Can you think of another word for the 'Underground'?
10. What happens at the Royal Albert Hall?
11. What are the two houses of Parliament?
12. Where would you find a Beefeater?

Intermediate

Students read the text and look closely at the photos. Do the quizzes on Teacher's Book pages 94-95.

Here's an extra idea
It's fun to explore the variety of words which we use to describe the same concept, e.g. 'The metal was put into the wall at 17°C because heat affects its size'. Metal gets bigger or smaller depending on temperature — the verbs used to describe this movement are 'expand' and 'contract'.

Mime pumping up a bicycle tyre and ask which verbs we use to describe this movement *(inflate)*, and ask for the opposite *(deflate)*.
Ask:

What about a woollen sweater?	*Stretch/shrink*
Numbers of students in a school?	*Increase/ decrease*
Weather temperatures?	*Rise/fall*

Advanced

1. The walk is approximately an hour long, through the heart of London's West End.
2. It goes through three distinctly different shopping areas.
3. We provide a photo-type quiz as preparation for the walk, and further vocabulary work which can be done before, during, or after the excursion.
4. After the initial 'work' the students should have a much better idea of the shopping facilities open to them, and can be let loose to get on with their own shopping.

Your map on Teacher's Book page 96 shows the walk.

Do the photo quiz before you attempt the walk so that the students already have an idea of what to look out for. (Answers on Teacher's Book page 97.)

When we did this walk, the following vocabulary and ideas were generated by our students.

Goods: every day goods/luxury goods/fruit 'n veg/trinkets and knick knacks/bargains/prices slashed/reduced/souvenirs.

Shopping: bargain-hunting/window-shopping/browsing/shop-lifting.

People: well-dressed/badly-dressed/smart/well-off/down and out/classy/elegant/harassed.

Words overhead: 'Mind yer backs', 'Keep yer flaming 'ands off', 'Come again, luv?'. 'Can I help you, Madam?'. 'Are you being served, Sir?'.

Streets and buildings: red-bricked/tucked-away/shabby/ornate/run down/up and coming/squalid/converted/pedestrianized.

Here are a couple of questions for the students to think about.

What differences do you notice between the buildings and shoppers in each area?
How do prices compare to your own country?

OUT AND ABOUT IN LONDON
Travelling around

Here are some pictures showing things that tourists often do in London. These pages are to help you read and understand signs which you will see in the city. Imagine you are in London yourself. Look at the pictures and answer the questions.

1. Many tourists have difficulties when they buy an Underground ticket. They often have to queue because they haven't got any change for the machines. So always carry 5p and 10p coins.

But there are other difficulties for the poor tourist. Look at what you have to do to buy a ticket from a machine and to get to the trains.

Can you put the photos in order and give easy instructions to anyone who doesn't know the underground?

2. This special bus (above) helps tourists. Where does it go to?

20

Answers:

1. Put the right money into the ticket machine
Take your ticket and put it into the slot at the barriers
When the barriers open, walk through
Take your ticket out of the top of the machine.

2. It goes to all the main shopping areas in London.

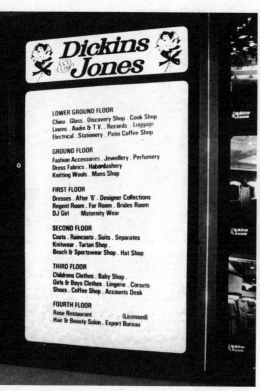

Dickins & Jones

LOWER GROUND FLOOR
China . Glass . Discovery Shop . Cook Shop
Linens . Audio & T.V. . Records . Luggage
Electrical . Stationery . Patio Coffee Shop

GROUND FLOOR
Fashion Accessories . Jewellery . Perfumery
Dress Fabrics . Haberdashery
Knitting Wools . Mans Shop

FIRST FLOOR
Dresses . After '6' . Designer Collections
Regent Room . Fur Room . Brides Room
DJ Girl   Maternity Wear

SECOND FLOOR
Coats . Raincoats . Suits . Separates
Knitwear . Tartan Shop .
Beach & Sportswear Shop . Hat Shop

THIRD FLOOR
Childrens Clothes . Baby Shop .
Girls & Boys Clothes . Lingerie . Corsets
Shoes . Coffee Shop . Accounts Desk

FOURTH FLOOR
Rose Restaurant   (Licensed)
Hair & Beauty Salon . Export Bureau

3. You take the bus and get off at Dickins and Jones. Look at this list of presents you want to buy for friends and relations at home.
a) Which floor and which department do you have to go to if you want to buy:

a Scottish kilt
a cassette recorder
a nightie
writing-paper

a cashmere sweater
a brooch
a souvenir tea-towel
swimming-trunks
a book of English recipes
a teapot.

b) You decide you need to sit down and have a good lunch and a glass of wine. Which floor do you go to?

4. After lunch you want to go sightseeing. You decide to go to the Tower of London but you're not sure that this is the right bus. What do you ask the conductor?

West End Cinemas

ABC 1 & 2 (QUEENSWAY) BAYSWATER.
1: EVERY WHICH WAY BUT LOOSE (AA)
2.40, 5.20, 7.55. Late show Fri & Sat 11.15.
2: SUPERMAN (A)
1.45, 4.25, 7.35. Late show Fri & Sat 11.15.

ABC EDGWARE ROAD.
SUPERMAN (A)
2.00, 5.10, 8.20. Progs 1.25, 4.35, 7.45. Late show Fri & Sat 11.15

ABC 1, 2, 3, 4 & 5 FULHAM ROAD.
SEATS BKBLE LAST SEP PERF. (Doors open 15 mins prior) Licensed Bar
1: SUPERMAN (A)
1.45, 4.40. Sep perf 8.15.

5. After your busy day, you decide to go to a film. You buy a paper and choose *Superman*. You know it's a popular film but you don't want to queue. You want to book in advance and arrange to meet a friend at the cinema for a drink before the film starts.
a) Which cinema do you choose?
b) When is the earliest time you can have a drink in the cinema?

6. If *Every Which Way But Loose were on at this cinema, could you take a 13-year-old to see it?*

21

4. Does this go to the Tower of London please?

5. a) ABC 1, Fulham Road.
b) 15 minutes before the film begins.

6. No.

---

3. a) kilt . . . Tartan shop on 2nd floor
recorder . . . audio and t.v. on Lower Ground Floor
nightie . . . lingerie on 3rd floor
writing paper . . . stationery on Lower Ground floor
sweater . . . knitwear on 2nd floor
brooch . . . jewellery on Ground Floor
tea towel . . . Cook Shop or Linens on Lower Ground Floor

swimming trunks . . . beach and sportswear on 2nd Floor
recipes . . . Cook Shop on Lower Ground Floor
teapot . . . china on Lower Ground Floor

b) 4th Floor

Give the students 3-4 minutes to study each photo and read the text. Close books. Students answer questions in writing, individually or in small groups. It's probably better to do the two quizzes on separate days.

OUT AND ABOUT IN LONDON

Piccadilly Circus

Where did this odd name come from? No-one really knows. One idea is that in the late sixteenth century, a man called Robert Baker used to make shirt "frills" in this area. These were called "pickadills". The local people nicknamed his house "Pickadilly Hall" and eventually the area became known as Piccadilly.

But why is it called a circus? Because the buildings around it used to be curved in the shape of a circle.

What's the name of the statue? That's Eros. *When and why was it built?* It was built in 1893 to honour Lord Shaftesbury who helped the local poor people. It represented his love and kindness.

At first, people were shocked because the statue had no clothes. This was no way to honour a Lord! Especially in 1893! It was soon nicknamed Eros, the Greek god of love – and the name has stayed ever since.

40

Questions:

Piccadilly Circus

1. How do you spell Piccadilly?
2. What's the name of the statue in the middle of Piccadilly Circus?
3. When was it built?
4. Why was it built?
5. What advertisements do you remember seeing?
6. Which way does the traffic go around the statue?
7. How many buses are in the picture?
8. What was a "pickadill"?
9. What did Lord Shaftesbury do?
10. Why is Piccadilly Circus called a circus?

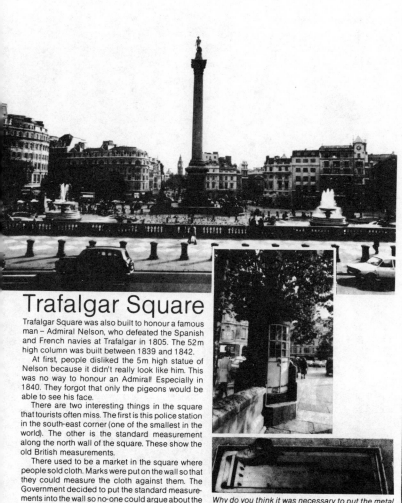

Trafalgar Square

Trafalgar Square was also built to honour a famous man – Admiral Nelson, who defeated the Spanish and French navies at Trafalgar in 1805. The 52 m high column was built between 1839 and 1842.

At first, people disliked the 5m high statue of Nelson because it didn't really look like him. This was no way to honour an Admiral! Especially in 1840. They forgot that only the pigeons would be able to see his face.

There are two interesting things in the square that tourists often miss. The first is this police station in the south-east corner (one of the smallest in the world). The other is the standard measurement along the north wall of the square. These show the old British measurements.

There used to be a market in the square where people sold cloth. Marks were put on the wall so that they could measure the cloth against them. The Government decided to put the standard measurements into the wall so no-one could argue about the length of a foot or a yard.

Why do you think it was necessary to put the metal into the wall at 62°F (17°C)?

Because of expansion and contraction.

41

Trafalgar Square

1. When was the Battle of Trafalgar?
2. What did people first think of Nelson's statue?
3. What's in the south-east corner of Trafalgar Square?
4. What's in the north wall of the square?
5. What used to be sold in the square?
6. How high is Nelson's Column?
7. When was it built?
8. Who can see Nelson's face today?
9. Which clock can you see?
10. Which fountain has the most water?

Detailed directions for the walk.

From Piccadilly Circus walk up Shaftesbury Avenue to the traffic lights at Rupert Street. Turn left and walk through Rupert Street market to Brewer Street. Cross Brewer Street and walk down the small passageway opposite you, passing Raymond's Revue Bar on your left. At the end of the passage, go straight on down Berwick Street market until you come to Broadwick Street. Turn left and continue to the end. Turn right and then first left and then right again into Carnaby Street. Walk down Carnaby Street until you come to the Shakespeare's Head on your left. Turn left down Foubert Street. At the end, turn left, then left again into Hamley's Toy Shop. Walk through the shop, up the stairs and cross over the street, through the covered passageway, to the main shop. Leave Hamley's by the main entrance which brings you into Regent Street. Turn right and walk to Oxford Circus. Then turn left and walk along to Old Bond Street. At Burlington Gardens, turn left and walk down Burlington Arcade which is on your right. This leads you into Piccadilly where you turn left and walk back to Piccadilly Circus.

OUT AND ABOUT IN LONDON
A shopping walk

Each of these comments goes with a photo – can you match them up?

a) I'm glad it's not your birthday every day of the week. Now make up your mind – what are you going to get?

b) I wonder what we'll get for it? I couldn't believe it when they said it was so old!

c) It's just over a pound but I'll only charge you 15p, love.

d) Round and round, every hour on the hour – it's enough to make you dizzy!

e) People don't usually see me, but I always see them. I've got such a good view from up here.

f) There's never a dull moment working round here, there's always somebody up to something.

g) Gee, what a lovely old fashioned store!

h) Looking at it now – you'd never believe it, would you?

The answers are:

a) = photo number   7
b)   2
c)   8
d)   4
e)   1
f)   3
g)   5
h)   6

61

GETTING EDUCATED

Annabel Evemy – schoolgirl

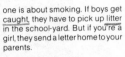

What age-group does your school take, Annabel?

Er...11 to 16 in the main school and 17 to 18-year-olds from next year.

Your school's called a Community College. Could you explain that?

Well, it just means that it's for everybody in the village to use, not just 11 to 18-year-olds. In fact, my mother studied sociology with the fifth form a couple of years ago.

Really, how did she get on?

Oh, she loved it, she got her O level! The school's open in the evenings as well, mostly for Adult Education classes...they learn all kinds of things: yoga, pottery, woodwork, local history. Some of the subjects are really interesting.

I always hated wearing school uniform when I was at school. Do you have to wear one?

Oh yes, the school's very strict about that...they think it makes us all look the same, so you can't tell which kids have well-off parents.

D'you think that's a good idea?

Yes, it's a good idea, but in fact, if they let us wear what we wanted, I'm sure we'd all wear jeans...

And what about other school rules – are there a lot of them?

No, not really, but the stupidest one is about smoking. If boys get caught, they have to pick up litter in the school-yard. But if you're a girl, they send a letter home to your parents.

And you don't think that's fair?

No, it's really unfair...they should do the same to all of us.

Is it the same in your lessons: do the boys study different things?

No, we all do woodwork and metalwork and art and – er – cookery, plus things like English and Maths up to the age of 14. Obviously– after that– people can choose.

What are your favourite subjects?

Oh, French and German– definitely!

Why's that?

Well, I enjoy learning languages. I love going abroad in the holidays – on exchange visits. I'm sure I learn more in a week abroad than in a year at school!

Really. How?

Just by speaking the language. All we do at school is learn grammar. We never say anything and the teachers always speak in English – actually, we don't think they can speak anything else!

You're probably right...But on the whole, do you like school?

Most of the time...yes!

22

A lot of students have problems with sound/spelling relationships in English. Five minute spelling tests are a good idea. Try this one, which uses words from the text — but make sure that the class is aware of this.

1. school
2. community
3. sociology
4. rules
5. litter
6. definitely
7. letter
8. cookery
9. wear
10. whole

| Aims | To provide a starting point for talking about and comparing different systems of education. |
| | To give intensive reading practice from the text. |

Aims

To provide a starting point for talking about and comparing different systems of education.
To give intensive reading practice from the text.

Background

A lot of holiday courses organise visits to local schools. These can be disastrous, especially at the lower language levels. Because the students know nothing about our school system, they have nothing to say when they meet English kids. This page gives some basic information about our educational system. It covers: school uniform; 'O' levels; school rules; the teaching of foreign languages. The text is a simplified version of an interview with Annabel Evemy who is now in the 5th form of Uplands Community College, Wadhurst, East Sussex.

Approach

Students read the interview.

Vocabulary questions.

Ask: **What do you think litter means? And well-off?**

Comprehension questions.
Ask: **Do the kids have to wear a uniform?**
       What happens to girls who are caught smoking?
       At what age can they choose what subjects to study?
       What are Annabel's favourite subjects?
       What's the difference between an ordinary school and a community college?

Extras

1.   Ask the class to look at timetable B on page 42 in the Student's Book and make some complete sentences from it.
2.   In nationality groups, the students can prepare mini lectures on their own school systems. Suggested headings for them to work on:
       — The school day.
       — What people wear.
       — Homework.
       — Exams.
       — School rules.
       — The teaching of foreign languages.

GETTING EDUCATED
Two timetables

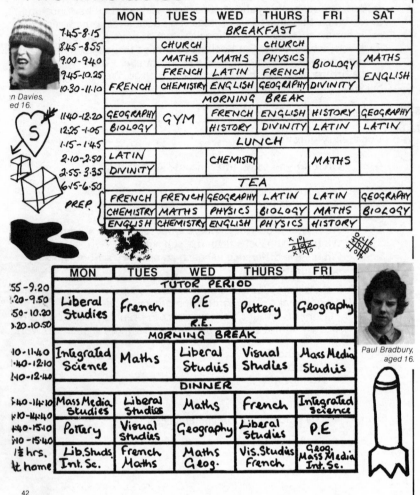

n Davies, ed 16.

	MON	TUES	WED	THURS	FRI	SAT
7.45-8.15	BREAKFAST					
8.45-8.55		CHURCH		CHURCH		
9.00-9.40		MATHS	MATHS	PHYSICS	BIOLOGY	MATHS
9.45-10.25		FRENCH	LATIN	FRENCH		ENGLISH
10.30-11.10	FRENCH	CHEMISTRY	ENGLISH	GEOGRAPHY	DIVINITY	
	MORNING BREAK					
11.40-12.20	GEOGRAPHY	GYM	FRENCH	ENGLISH	HISTORY	GEOGRAPHY
12.25-1.05	BIOLOGY		HISTORY	DIVINITY	LATIN	LATIN
1.15-1.45	LUNCH					
2.10-2.50	LATIN		CHEMISTRY		MATHS	
2.55-3.35	DIVINITY					
6.15-6.50	TEA					
PREP.	FRENCH	FRENCH	GEOGRAPHY	LATIN	LATIN	GEOGRAPHY
	CHEMISTRY	MATHS	PHYSICS	BIOLOGY	MATHS	BIOLOGY
	ENGLISH	CHEMISTRY	ENGLISH	PHYSICS	HISTORY	

	MON	TUES	WED	THURS	FRI
55-9.20	TUTOR PERIOD				
.20-9.50	Liberal Studies	French	P.E / R.E.	Pottery	Geography
.50-10.20					
.20-10.50					
	MORNING BREAK				
10-11.40	Integrated Science	Maths	Liberal Studies	Visual Studies	Mass Media Studies
.40-12.10					
.10-12.40					
	DINNER				
5.40-14.10	Mass Media Studies	Liberal Studies	Maths	French	Integrated Science
.10-14.40					
.40-15.10	Pottery	Visual Studies	Geography	Liberal Studies	P.E
.10-15.40					
1½ hrs. at home	Lib.Studs. Int.Sc.	French Maths	Maths Geog.	Vis.Studies French	Geog. Mass Media Int.Sc.

Paul Bradbury, aged 16.

42

Liberal Studies includes law and order; the role of the police force in society; the history of child labour; the family.

Integrated Science includes general science; physics, chemistry; biology — and lots of practical work in all these subjects.

Mass Media Studies includes how radio, t.v. and newspapers work; who runs them and how; advertising.

Visual Studies is a course which concentrates on 2 and 3 dimensional design work.

Quick Time Test

Ask the students to put the following times into 24 hour clock numbers:

Day time: quarter to four; twenty five to one; ten past ten; thirteen minutes past nin

Night time: twenty past seven; half past twelve; five past five; eleven minutes to eight.

Reverse by calling out **24 hour clock** times and getting the students to call them back in the normal conversational English way.

Aims	To highlight some of the differences between comprehensive and public school education, by making deductions from two sample timetables.
	To give practice in scanning tabulated information.
Background	Some private schools in Britain are called 'public' schools. The cost of sending a child to such a school can be as much as £3,000 a year. Comprehensive education is 'free', and paid for by the State through taxation. Both timetables are authentic: timetable A comes from Bradfield College, a public school in Berkshire; timetable B is from Connah's Quay High School in North Wales.

Approach Don't give the students any background information at this stage. Students work in groups.

Ask: **What can you say about these two schools by looking at the timetables.**
Give a 5 minute time limit.

List one point at a time from each group on the board in note form.

If necessary, guide their deductions.

Ask: **Which boy do you think works harder?**
What do 'R.E.' and 'P.E.' mean? *Religious Education and Physical Education.*

Which subjects do both boys do?

Ask for complete sentences from some of the notes on the board.
Now give the students the background information about schools in Britain and ask them to say which timetable refers to which school.
Make sure the class knows the following vocabulary:
boarding school/fee-paying/day school/ comprehensive/single (double, treble) period.

 Give students a minute to decide which timetable they would prefer to follow. Take a vote and then divide the class into two groups. Give students five minutes to prepare arguments in favour of their choice.

 Hold a short debate.

Extra *Scanning quiz*

Fire the following questions at the class. Students write down the answers. (See opposite.)
1. How long does Dan Davies have to eat his lunch?
2. How many French lessons does Paul Bradbury have per week?
3. What's Paul's last lesson of the week?
4. What's Dan doing when Paul goes to see his tutor on Thursdays?
5. Which subject does Dan do the most?
6. On which evening might Paul read or write about 'the role of television advertising in *Britain'?*
7. Who has the longer morning break?
8. When does Dan change his clothes for class?
9. What's Paul doing when Dan's studying chemistry immediately after lunch?
10. What subject does Paul study the least?

Students exchange books and mark each other's.

GETTING EDUCATED
Alternative ideas

The school day at the White Lion School, Islington, North London.

The White Lion school was set up as an alternative to State education; it is called a "free school" because the children are not forced to conform to any adult's definition of discipline or learning. They are free to choose what and how they want to learn.

The school opens when the first child arrives, usually at 8.45 am, but the children can arrive when they like. Most of them are in school by ten. Between nine and ten most people are in the living-room and the kitchen downstairs. Many of the children haven't had much breakfast so there is a lot of tea-drinking and toast-making and talking. This is a time when children and adults can work out what they are to do for the day.

By about ten most of the children are busily doing something but not every child will want to be involved immediately. Some of them will want to play and others will sit and read the papers.

On a typical morning in June two children were in the living-room, an adult was making the lunch and a parent was in the office answering the phone. Two children had just arrived and were talking on the stairs. Two were icing cakes in the nursery.

In the pottery-room, one of the older girls was finishing off a pot. Some children were in the maths-and-science room making model aeroplanes. Six children were upstairs; two were working on a project concerning their flats and the others were reading and drawing. Four of the older boys were on their way to Hornchurch Cardrome for driving lessons.

During the morning one adult,

THE ULTIMATE OBJECTIVE OF SCHOOL IS TO PRODUCE A CITIZEN — THAT IS TO CONTROL THE CHILD. EVEN HIS NATURAL ENJOYMENT OF PLAY IS USED TO SOCIALISE HIM.

LARRY DID THE BEST FINGERPAINTING. WHAT A GOOD BOY. YOUR MOTHER WILL BE PROUD OF YOU.

THE BEST TEACHERS WILL OF COURSE TRY TO FIND THINGS THAT TRULY INTEREST THE CHILD.

IT'S EASIER TO KEEP THEM IN ORDER THAT WAY AT LEAST.

BUT THE ULTIMATE TEST IS WHETHER THE CHILD WOULD FREELY CHOOSE TO GO TO SCHOOL.

SCHOOLS OUT, SCHOOLS OUT, TEACHER'S LET THE FOOLS OUT.

NO MORE PENCILS, NO MORE BOOKS, NO MORE TEACHER'S DIRTY LOOKS.

IF NOT, IT IS COERCION HOWEVER SUBTLE

AND THE CHILD SPENDS MOST OF HIS WAKING HOURS IN THIS ENVIRONMENT.

OR DOING HOMEWORK FOR IT.

OF COURSE SOME CHILDREN ESCAPE

SURE I GO TO SCHOOL MAN — SOMETIMES.

usually helped by several children, makes the lunch. There is a rota-system for jobs like this so that everyone gets a chance to do the lunch about once a week. Lunch is served at around one o'clock and is eaten in the living room. After lunch it is someone else's turn to do the washing-up. This is a very unpopular job and most of the children are reluctant to help. As the adults are also reluctant to do it on their own, they usually reach a compromise. After lunch, the children carry on with their activities until 4.30.

On Mondays, Tuesdays and Thursdays the school is open in the evenings until 9 pm. The same kind of activities continue during the evenings. On Tuesday evening the school is also open to visitors between 7 and 9 pm. On Wednesday afternoon and evening there is a school meeting. On Friday there is no evening school but occasionally there is an outside activity planned, such as a visit to the cinema. The school is also open every weekend.

62

Ask your students to give one word for the following phrasal verbs from the text. (Possible answers in brackets.)

to set up	(to establish)
to work out	(to plan)
to finish off	(to complete)
to carry on with	(to continue)

Aims	To give information about 'progressive' educational ideas and ways in which they are being put into practice in Great Britain. To give the students an opportunity to give their opinions of the course and to suggest ways of improving future courses. To teach some of the language used when making polite criticisms.
Background	In many ways, a holiday language course is the only alternative form of education that the students will ever encounter. Compared to the White Lion school, it's a fairly weak alternative, but the mixture of holiday and learning combined with the different expectations of leaders, students, parents, teachers and course organisers can lead to a good deal of friction. For the teacher, the most important people are the students. This text should provide a lead-in to a more general discussion of the educational experience they have just had.

Approach

 Students read cartoon. Ask for any reactions.

 List on the board the main features of the education that your students have received, as well as some general facts about education in their countries, for example:
Do they have nursery schools? What age?
When do most people start school?
When do they specialise in certain subjects?
What exams are taken and when?
What proportion (if any) of schools are private?
Who decides what the students do and when?
How much choice do they have in their educational systems?

Introduce more general themes.
Ask: **Some children hate school — in what ways do they show it?**
Elicit/teach: to play truant/truancy/to vandalise things/graffiti.
What happens to difficult children?

Talk about the students' opinions of their own education.
Ask: **What were the good points of your education? And the bad?**
How could it have been improved?

Students read the text. Point out that this school caters for children who have proved to be too much of a problem in the ordinary state schools.

 Reactions to the text?
Ask: **What specific things in the school identify it as an alternative system of education?**
Do you agree with these differences, or do you think they could bring problems?
Are there any similarities between the White Lion School and a holiday language course?
What do you think the aims of a holiday course should be?
Have these been fulfilled in your case?
If not, how do you think the course could be improved in the future?

Extra

Students write their ideal timetable for a week on a holiday language course, indicating the proportion of work vs holiday, and what they would like to do during these times.

LOOKING AHEAD
Reading tea leaves

All foreigners know that the British spend most of their time drinking tea. There are three reasons for this: firstly, we're a thirsty nation; secondly, we don't know how to make coffee; and thirdly, we believe we can read the future in the tea leaves at the bottom of our empty cups.

This explains why the traditional British cuppa is never made with teabags. So, put the kettle on and relax! We're going to reveal the secret world of the British tea-drinker...

When you finish your cup of tea, empty it into the saucer and, keeping the cup upside down, turn it round three times clockwise.

Now you need the expert skills of the teacup reader who looks for signs in the patterns in your cup.

Imagine you're reading your friend's teacup. The first things to look for are "tears". Take the cup from your friend and look to see if any tea is running down the inside. Sometimes there are a lot of "tears", sometimes only a few, and sometimes none at all. What do you think they mean?

Next you must try to see patterns in the cup. Here are some of the most usual ones: question-marks, bridges, roads and hills. All these things mean future problems for your friend.

Spiders are very bad news: tell your friend that someone she likes

will disappoint her. After that, she won't want to be friends with that person.

Look for initials in the cup: they can tell you more about the problems. Ask your friend if she knows anyone whose name begins with any of the letters you can see.

You don't just want to look for bad news, so look carefully into the cup. Can you see a bird flying near the edge? This means good news from abroad will come soon.

Lots of birds can mean foreign travel in the near future.

Don't forget to look for these if you're both going home soon – she'll be astonished at your intelligence!

Tiny tea-leaves, which look like dust, scattered around the cup mean that your friend will get some money soon. The more there are, the more money she'll get.

Finally, if you can see a hammer, this is very good because it shows that your friend will have success in something that's very important to her.

Look carefully at the cup shown here. Can you read the secrets in it? Change what you **see** into what you **say** about the future.

Initials:

Ask your students to find out the meanings of the following well-known ones:

BBC/VAT/A.A./H.R.H./U.K./V.H.F./ P.O./I.B.M./I.R.A.

23

Aim	To talk about the future, using 'will' to express predictions and speculations.
Background	Grammar note: there are at least six ways of expressing the future in English. At this level, students should be able to use the present continuous and 'going to' forms to talk about their future plans. This page should help to put this particular use of 'will' into their active vocabulary.
	Pronunciation note: encourage the class to contract 'will' and 'will not' as in 'she'll' and 'she won't'

Approach Students read the first three paragraphs.

Vocabulary questions.

Ask: **What's another word for nation?**
What does 'cuppa' mean?
And clockwise?

Comprehension questions.

Ask: **Why do the British drink a lot of tea?**
What can you do with the tea leaves at the bottom of the cup?

Students read the rest of the text. Pre-teach vocabulary you think they will have difficulty with: spider/dust/astonished.

Write on the board: bridges/roads
birds
dust
Point to one of the board cues.

Ask: **You see this in my cup. What does it mean?**
You'll get some good news
Practise the contraction 'You'll'
Practise with the other cues: birds/dust

Point out that 'won't' is the contraction for 'will not'.
Practise with verbal cues:

Say:	**Good luck**	*You won't have good luck.*
	A lot of money	*You won't get a lot of money.*
	Problems	*You won't have problems.*
	Travel abroad	*You won't travel abroad.*

Students look at the photo and write what they think the tea-leaves show.

 Some of the students read their predictions out — the rest of the class agree or disagree.

Extras

1. Teach some verbs and adverbs which express specualtion and opinion, for example:
I think/I feel sure/I suppose/maybe/probably/perhaps.
Ask the students to think about what will happen when they arrive back in their own countries.
Help by giving cues if necessary.

Say: **parents/meet/airport**
sister/happy/see me
watch/favourite programme/t.v.

Quickly go round class getting at least one sentence from each student.

2. *General discussion point*
Ways of telling the future in their own countries. Do this either as an informal ten minute chat, or put them into nationality groups to prepare mini-lectures to give to the rest of the class.

LOOKING AHEAD

Reading palms

Kathy McKay has worked on Hastings pier for 14 years. She prefers reading palms because she thinks that they give a more accurate reading of the future than Tarot cards or crystal balls. When she started, most of her clients were women – today, just as many are men.

She always looks at both palms because the left one shows your real character while the right one shows the character you would like people to think you have!

Here are some of the things she told us about reading palms:

When the Finger of Jupiter is very long, it means you are big-headed and bossy.

A square, fat Finger of Saturn shows a serious-minded person. A pointed one shows a more light-hearted kind of person.

People who have a long Finger of Sun, one that's almost as long as the Finger of Jupiter are creative and artistic – they are the ones who want to "get to the top".

When the Finger of Mercury is long and well-shaped it shows a born leader.

The lines on the palm are very important:

When the Line of Fate is clearly marked, it shows that you're going to be well-off. What do you think it means if it isn't marked clearly?

A strong Line of Heart indicates that you are warm-hearted. A weak line shows that you are tight-fisted.

A strong Line of Head shows that you're brainy. What do you think a weak line shows?

Nervous people have a strong girdle of Venus.

Look at the length of the line of marriage. A long line shows a long and happy marriage. What about a broken line?

Look what Kathy McKay wrote about this person. What's going to happen to her?

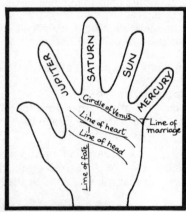

General questions:

Ask your students what they think a pier is. (If necessary, refer them to the drawing on Student's Book page 53.)
Why do they think they were built?
When do they think they were built?

Aim	To introduce and practise new vocabulary, especially words and phrases used to describe personality.
Background	If you're teaching in, or planning to visit, a resort which has a pier, your students might be interested in the following information.

Piers first became popular in the 1870s. There were two reasons for this: first, paddle steamers which toured the coast needed deep water to unload their crew and passengers, and it was easier to build piers into the sea rather than make deep harbours to accomodate them. Second, sea-air became the fashionable 'cure' for all kinds of ailments, so seaside towns grew in popularity. Before this, mineral waters had been the universal panacea, but now spa towns like Bath, Cheltenham, Tunbridge Wells and Leamington declined and were replaced by Brighton, Blackpool, Bournemouth, Eastbourne and Hastings. The pier at Hastings was opened in 1872 after three years' work, at a cost of £23,000. It is still privately owned and about 400,000 visitors stroll along its wooden deck every year.

Approach

Elicit/teach the following vocabulary by pointing to parts of your hand:
back of the hand
palm of the hand
thumb/index finger/middle finger/ring finger/little finger
nails/knuckles/wrist/fist
('Bunch of fives' and 'knuckle sandwich' are fun to teach!)
Lead into compound adjectives: tight-fisted (mean with money), open-handed (generous).
Show how they are formed and pronounced — with the stress on 'fist' and 'hand'

Students read through text and identify compound adjectives. They should try to work out the meanings.

Ask for the meanings of:
bossy
get to the top
born leader
well-off
brainy

Students look at each other's palms and write a short paragraph on what they can see in each of them.

Students look at the photo of Kathy McKay's chart and make complete sentences from the information on it.

Extra

If you're teaching at a seaside resort which has a palmist, you could suggest that one or two of the students have their palms read. If possible, they should tape-record the reading, which would provide you with authentic listening material. If not, ask them to note what the palmist says, especially about each finger and the palm lines. The information can then be compared with Kathy McKay's system of reading palms. How similar are they? What are the major differences?

LOOKING AHEAD

About time

In my lifetime
Time and time again
People have said:
  "Don't waste time
  Don't get out of time
  Stay in time
  Get there on time
  Don't be small-time
  Hit the big time"

Timely advice
To a time-waster
Like me
In the meantime
Killing time
Takes up all of my time

They say: "Time flies
When you're having fun"
In my case
Finding spare time
Is a question of timing

In no time
I'll be saying:
"Why did I waste time?
Why did I take so much time
  off?"
Time's funny
It's never here
It's either coming or it's gone

63

An alternative version:

During my life
Frequently
People have said:
"Don't hang around
Don't get out of step
Keep up to date
Be punctual
Don't think small
Be successful"

Useful advice
To a lazy person
Like me
Meanwhile
Doing nothing
Keeps me busy

They say: "The hours go quickly
When you're having fun"
In my case
Finding spare moments
Needs careful planning

Very soon
I'll be saying:
"Why did I miss my chances
Why didn't I work harder?"
Time's funny
It's never here
It's either coming or it's gone

Aims	To teach idiomatic language associated with time. To give practice in precise descriptive language and language used in forming hypotheses.
Background	It's always good to have one or two different things up your sleeve to use towards the end of the course. Here are two ideas that we have enjoyed using with advanced groups. They seem to work well because they tempt the students into using their own initiative and also allow you to act as adviser rather than teacher.

Approach Books closed. Read the poem out aloud. Ask for comments on the general 'feeling'.
Books open. Read the poem again while students follow text.

 In groups of three, students re-write the poem, using the word 'time' once only. (See opposite.)
Go round the groups answering questions, feeding in language as required.

 Students read their own poems to each other.

Extra

DUTS

The aim of this activity is to get the students to supply a definition of the word 'DUT'.

Draw figure 1 on the board; ask them to describe the relationship of the shapes, for example:
There's a square, a circle and a triangle.
The square is to the right of the circle, the triangle is to the left. The square is not touching the circle but the triangle is intersecting it.
Check that they know the following: right angle/circumference/right-angled triangle, etc.
Tell them that figure 1 is a DUT .
Ask for ideas on what constitiutes a DUT.

Draw figure 2 and repeat the descriptive process; ask for more hypotheses on the nature of a DUT. Finally, tell them that this is also a DUT.
Continue in the same way with the rest of the shapes, grouping and re-grouping the students physically, according to their hypotheses. Once they realise what a DUT is, ask them to write a precise definition of the word, suitable for inclusion in a dictionary.

Answer: Figs 3 & 6 are the only ones that aren't DUTS. A DUT is any combination of a circle, a right-angled triangle and a square, in which the two sides of the triangle containing the right angle are parallel to two sides of the square.

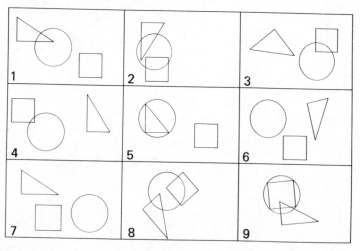

Make and take home

These pages give a few practical suggestions for making things which can be taken home as presents for family and friends. They can also provide you with interesting teaching material. Obviously, they are not morning class activities, but you may find that you can take small groups off in the afternoons, while the rest of the students are involved in sports or other organised activities.

You'll find that the ideas on these pages speak for themselves. The language is graded so your students should be able to use them as a reference and guide without your help, but if you find that some elementary students are interested in making brass rubbings, for example, use more advanced students to explain the basic instructions to them.

If you enjoy making things yourself, use your own ideas — but try to choose things that can be completed in an afternoon session in order to keep motivation high.

MAKE AND TAKE HOME
Badges and fudge

How to make "Ye Olde Englishe Fudge"

You need: 225g butter, 1kg sugar, a large tin of condensed milk, a cup of ordinary milk, vanilla essence, a saucepan with a heavy bottom.

First melt the butter and the ordinary milk in the saucepan.

Add the sugar and let it dissolve slowly.

After that, boil for five minutes, stirring all the time.

Add the condensed milk and boil everything for about another 15 minutes.

Take a small amount of the boiling fudge and put it into a saucer of cold water.

If it stays soft in the water, it's ready.

Then remove from the heat, add the vanilla and beat with a wooden spoon for two or three minutes.

Pour into a dish and leave to cool. Cut into small pieces to take home.

Make to how a badge British

Empty it

Keep it flat with a wooden spoon

Keep the heat very low

Watch carefully – things happen fast

Take a crisp or a peanut packet

As it gets smaller, keep turning the bag over

Or use some glue to fix the pin to the back

Make it flat and put it under an electric or gas grill

When the bag is the size you want, remove it from the grill

Put a safety-pin through the back of the badge while it's still warm.

24

An acceptable order is:

How to make a British badge.

Take a crisp or a peanut packet.
Empty it.
Make it flat and put it under an electric or gas grill.
Keep the heat very low.
Watch carefully — things happen fast.
As it gets smaller, keep turning the bag over.
Keep it flat with a wooden spoon.

When the bag is the size you want, remove it from the grill.
Put a safety-pin through the back of the badge while it's still warm.
Or use some glue to fix the pin to the back.

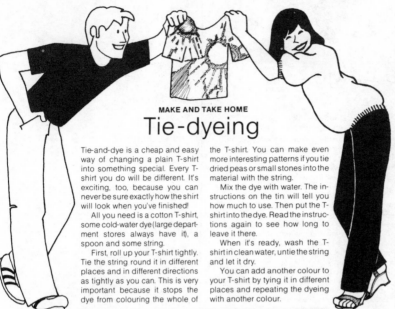

MAKE AND TAKE HOME

Tie-dyeing

Tie-and-dye is a cheap and easy way of changing a plain T-shirt into something special. Every T-shirt you do will be different. It's exciting, too, because you can never be sure exactly how the shirt will look when you've finished!

All you need is a cotton T-shirt, some cold-water dye (large department stores always have it), a spoon and some string.

First, roll up your T-shirt tightly. Tie the string round it in different places and in different directions as tightly as you can. This is very important because it stops the dye from colouring the whole of the T-shirt. You can make even more interesting patterns if you tie dried peas or small stones into the material with the string.

Mix the dye with water. The instructions on the tin will tell you how much to use. Then put the T-shirt into the dye. Read the instructions again to see how long to leave it there.

When it's ready, wash the T-shirt in clean water, untie the string and let it dry.

You can add another colour to your T-shirt by tying it in different places and repeating the dyeing with another colour.

Potato Prints

Tie and dye is fun because you get a surprise at the end, but you might prefer to have more control over the way you dye your clothes. Potato prints are also easy to do, but if you are careful, you can get very neat results.

Slice a potato in half, then cut out a design on it (see diagram). Then fill your T-shirt completely with crumpled newspaper to stop the dye from going on to the parts you don't want dyed. Dip the potato into the dye and press it carefully on to the T-shirt.

Leave it to dry completely, then put it into a mixture of cold water and salt. This fixes the dye and stops it from colouring the rest of the T-shirt when you wash it.

What other designs can the students come up with? Teach the language they'll need: diamonds/circles/squares/triangles/rectangles.

You could also teach some of the more unusual names of colours: lemon/tangerine/purple/scarlet/violet.

And some compound colours: shocking pink/chocolate brown/pillar-box red/navy blue.

N.B. The free colour charts put out by paint manufacturers are really useful for this.

44

MAKE AND TAKE HOME

Brass rubbing

A rubbing is made by placing a piece of paper over a metal or stone object that has indentations. Wax is then rubbed over the paper until an image of the object shows on it. The rubbing can then be framed and put on a wall like a picture. Why not try making one and taking it home as a present?

All you need is some white lining-paper, which you can buy from a wallpaper shop, and wax. Heel-ball wax is the best and you can get it from most shoe-repair shops. It comes in sticks, best for delicate objects, or cakes, fine for bigger rubbings.

The most popular types of rubbings are of brass memorial stones which were used to cover graves. They are usually likenesses of the dead person and were most popular from the 13th to the 15th Centuries. You can find them in old churches, but because of the damage that could be caused by enthusiastic but inexperienced rubbers, many vicars now refuse permission for them to be rubbed. In order to preserve existing brasses, yet still encourage rubbing, centres around Britain have been set up where you can go and learn how to do it by using reproduction brasses.

If you don't feel like starting with something as big as a church brass, look around the streets of any town. There are all kinds of interesting objects that make lovely rubbings.

Some people enjoy rubbing coal-hole covers! Most of these were made in the mid-19th Century. They were designed to fit into the road and cover up the holes leading to the cellars where coal was stored. When a family needed more coal, the cover was lifted up and the coal was poured directly into the cellar below. If you look at the covers closely, you'll see they have an amazing variety of designs: stars, crosses, circles, squares and even snow-flakes.

Post-boxes are good too. They all have on them the initials (called ciphers) of the reigning monarch of the time they were made, so you can get interesting historical rubbings from them.

There are a lot of different ways to get your rubbing but the easiest is just to put your piece of white paper over the object (make sure this is clean by rubbing it first with a cloth), fix it with tape or weight it down with books. Then start to rub hard with the wax. Always rub in the same direction. Take your time and rub only in sections. Don't worry if you go over the edges, most rubbings are cut out and then stuck on to a thicker piece of paper or card.

When you've finished, take a piece of nylon (old tights are good) and polish the surface of the rubbing until the wax shines. White paper and black wax produce a negative image. A positive one is easy to make too – use white paper and ordinary white candle wax. Rub in the way described above and polish with nylon. When you get home, lie the rubbing flat and weight the edges. Then soak a sponge in water, squeeze out and dip into a saucer of black Indian ink. Quickly and lightly go over the rubbing with this. As the ink penetrates the unwaxed parts it will fill in as a dark background leaving an ivory coloured object. Wipe off excess ink with a tissue and leave it to dry.

Roll up your rubbings carefully and put them into cardboard tubes so that you can carry them home safely and mount them there.

Impression of a finished brass rubbing. The original version was several feet high.

BRASS RUBBING CENTRES

Bath
The Friends Meeting House
York St. (off Abbey Church Yard)

Bristol
St. Nicholas Church and City Museum
Baldwin St.

Cambridge
Wesley Church Library
King St.

Canterbury
Sidney Cooper Building
St. Peter's St. (near Westgate)

Chichester
The Cloisters
Chichester Cathedral

Coventry
The Cathedral
Wyley Chapel

Dodington
Dodington House
Gloucestershire

Edinburgh
Canongate Tolbooth
Royal Mile
and
St. John's Church
Princes' St.

Glastonbury
St. John's Church
High Street

Gloucester
The Cathedral

London
All Hallow's Church
Byward St.
EC3 (next to Tower of London)

Greenwich Brass Rubbing Centre
15 Nelson Road
SE10

St. George's Church
Aubrey Walk
off Campden Hill
W8

St. James's Church
Piccadilly
W1

Westminster Abbey
Cloisters

Marlborough
St. Peter's Church

Newcastle upon Tyne
Laing Art Gallery

Nottingham
St. Mary's Church
High Pavement
The Lacemarket

Oxford
University Church of St. Mary the Virgin
High Street
and
The Museum of Oxford
St. Aldates

Winchester
The Museum (near Cathedral)

Windsor
St. John the Baptist
High Street (next to the Guildhall)

Woodstock
Oxford County Museum

More on games

The following selection of games are ones which we have played successfully with our own classes, and we hope that some of them will be new to you. Most of them are not specifically EFL games so this may encourage you to adapt your own games for classroom use.

Those marked * are the ones that we feel are more suited, linguistically, to higher levels.

Another source of EFL games is: 'Take Five,' published by the Centre for British Teachers, Head Street, Colchester, Essex.

The name game

Useful for teachers who have problems remembering their students' names! You and the class stand in a circle. Begin by saying your own name, then the student on your right says his/hers and so on round the circle. Then whisper your name; the student on your left whispers his/hers and so on round the circle. Repeat but this time shout your name. With more advanced classes continue by instructing the students to say their names in the way they'd like other people to say them. Then ask them to say their name in a way that expresses their innermost fantasies!

Human knots

A good ice-breaker for your first lesson with a new class. You should all link hands in a large circle. No-one should let go of anyone else's hands until the activity is over. Then begin to tie yourselves into knots by going under and over any available hands and arms. Shout STOP when everybody is tied up; then, still holding hands, disentangle yourselves.

Variation: Make two circles, one inside the other — this way makes more complicated knots.

Group instructions

Give two or three students a drawing like the one below; ask them to work out instructions for getting into this position. They should then give the instructions to the other students, who remain seated until they have heard them all. They then stand up and arrange themselves according to the instructions received. In groups, students then work out different positions and instructions and practise them on each other.

Murder!

Prepare as many slips of paper as there are students in your class. Mark one with a black dot and one with a black cross. The students move around, while you walk around giving out the papers. You should explain before-hand that the student who gets the one with the spot is the murderer, and that he/she murders people by winking at them. The one who gets the cross is the detective. The students group round in a circle with the detective in the centre, scanning the circle looking for the murderer. If any student is winked at by the murderer, he/she must fall down dead. The detective has only three 'goes' to find the murderer.

Vocabulary testing

The following activity is better when done in small groups rather than with the class as a whole.

Revision of recently-learned vocabulary can be done by prepared cards on which you have written the new words. Give a card to a student who then has to get the meaning of the word over to the rest of the class, without actually saying the word, for example:
cassette recorder.
Student says 'You use it when you want to listen to music'
Class guesses 'Stereo'

Student says 'No, it's smaller, you can carry it with you'

Or: Split the class into two teams, and give out cards containing recently-learned words. One student shouts out a word and challenges one from the other group to respond with a full sentence using it correctly. Award points for correct answers.

Or: At higher levels, check your class's ability to use new vocabulary and idioms by putting items up on the board and asking them, in pairs, to construct a story using all the words.

Group extension*

Divide the class into groups of roughly equal numbers, each with a leader. The leader asks a question — each person in the group replies but no reply can be the same, for example:

Leader	Who's the baker?
A	I don't know.
B	I am.
C	Not me.
D	Percy is.

The person on the leader's right becomes the next leader and asks the next question, which should be based on the language area already established, for example:

Leader When will the baker finish his work? When this game gets going, some interesting bits of conversation start to emerge.

Word association *

Here, a story line is established around the class. No student must use more than three words, for example.

A	Peter is the . . .
B	. . . idiot of this . . .
C	. . . group which never . . .
D	. . . seems to establish . . .

This can also be done as a written exercise.

Deduction games

In the following, the students have to deduce the rules of the games from the examples given by you. Let another student into the 'secret' before you start, so that the rest of the class have two examples to exercise their powers of logic on.

a) **Double letters**
Start by giving a couple of sentences as examples:
'It can be the moon but not the stars'.
'It can be green but not blue'.

Ask the student you have chosen to help you to give a sentence, then the rest of the class should start to call out sentences which you and your helper judge. Feed in more sentences to help them as the game continues, for example:
'It can be in foot but not in toe.'
'It can be in knee but not in elbow.'
The students who work out the 'secret' should begin producing their own sentences but keep their discovery secret from those who haven't yet got it.

b) **The moon is round . . .**
This is similar to 'Double letters' but this time, the 'secret' is the cough you do each time before saying the following sentence: 'The moon is round, has two eyes, a nose and a mouth'. You can 'draw' the moon and its features in the air when you say the sentence to provide a red herring. Again, you and your helper are the judges of whether the class's sentences are correct. Usually some players unwittingly clear their throats before saying their sentence and so are completely baffled to find that their sentences are 'correct' one time and then not the following time.

c) **My auntie went to Paris. . .**
In this game, you and your helper complete the sentence by adding nouns which begin with the initial letter of your first name, for example:
'My auntie went to Paris and brought back some lollipops'.

Variation: begin the noun with the last letter of the previous object e.g. sausages — sugar — rice — eggs

Make the game more difficult for higher levels by putting an adjective, starting with the same letter, in front of the noun, for example:
'My auntie went to Paris and brought back some lovely lollipops'.

E.F.L. Scrabble

Divide the class into groups, and divide the scrabble letters equally between them. One person from each group turns over a letter in turn. When someone spots a word, they have to say it, spell it and then put it into a sentence. The group can then keep the word.

Points are deducted for spelling or concept mistakes — 1 or ½ depending on the error, As the game continues, each group can add letters to other groups' words to make longer words. If they do it successfully, the word becomes their own. Add up the points on the Scrabble letters at the end and deduct points lost for errors.

Botticelli*

A good test of general knowledge, best played with culturally homogenous classes. One person decides to 'be' a famous person; thinks: 'I'll be Karl Marx'. He/she then tells the rest of the class the initial: 'My name begins with M'.

Either individually or together, the class then thinks of famous people whose names begin with M, e.g. Marilyn Monroe, Manet. Then they must ask indirect questions about the identity of the person — not, for example: 'Are you Marilyn Monroe?', but 'Were you a famous American Film star?'

The first player has to give any correct answer which fits the question, for example: 'No, I'm not Marilyn Monroe'. (although there may be other famous stars whose names are equally acceptable).

The next question could be: 'Were you a famous French painter?' If the first player can't think of one in reply, the class can then ask a question *about* the person, but it can only be answered by 'yes' or 'no', for example: 'Are you alive?' 'No'.

The game continues up to 20 questions and the person who guesses correctly can choose who to 'be' in the next round.

If you were . . .

In this game, a student thinks of a famous person and the others have to guess his/her identity in no more than 20 questions by asking questions like this:

1st player	Decides to be the Pope.
Class asks	If you were a country, what would you be?
1st player	Italy/Poland (both valid).
Class	If you were a car, what would you be?
1st player	A Fiat.
Class	If you were a colour, what would you be?
1st player	Purple.

E.F.L. charades

Divide the class into two approximately equal teams. Each group discusses and decides on the same number of items as there are members of the opposing team. These items can be: book titles/film titles/song titles/t.v. programmes/ short, well-known lines of poetry or prose.

They should write each on a separate slip of paper. The first member of the opposing team comes over and is given one. He/she looks at it, puts it away and then attempts to mime it to his/her own team. They guess, and the student doing the mime has to encourage guesses along the right lines and discourage wrong ones using the following gestures: nod or thumbs up for 'correct'; shake head for 'wrong'; beckon with hands for 'carry on in that direction or with that line of thought'.

There are various accepted gestures that the student can use to guide his/her own team. Make sure that all the students understand and remember them before they start doing their mimes. The most common are outlined below.

Identifying the genre.
Book: mime opening a book, hands together, palms upwards.
Song: one hand on chest, one hand out-stretched, mouth open.
Film: mime holding a camera and winding the handle.
T.V. programme: mime a screen by drawing it in the air with the forefingers.
Poem/prose: back of one hand on forehead, other hand writing

Identifying the number of words in the sentence.
Simply hold up the right number of fingers. Students should indicate which word they're beginning with by pointing to a finger, or, if they want to mime the whole thing at once, they sketch a circle in the air.

Identifying which syllable of a particular word is going to be mimed.
Using the three parts of the index finger, hit the corresponding part with another finger.

Sounds like . . .
If the word is difficult to mime, they can use the 'sound like' technique. Mime an easier word that rhymes with the one in the sentence or title, but precede it by the gesture of cupping an ear, e.g. to get 'this', cup ear to elicit 'sounds like' from team, then mime 'kiss'.

The team then quickly runs through words that rhyme with 'kiss' until they get 'this'.

The . . . a . . . etc.
There is also a symbol for 'the' which is simply putting one forefinger horizontally on top of the other to make the shape of a T. Small words like 'a' 'at' 'by' etc. are indicated by holding the thumb and forefinger close together. The team then calls out small words until it gets the right one.

Don't be put off by the length of these instructions. You can teach the gestures very quickly, even to elementary classes. The main problem with charades is that students get addicted to it — so never play it at the beginning of a session!

The adverb game

Useful for revision. One student leaves the class, while the others think of an adverb, e.g. slowly, loudly, elegantly, enigmatically (depending on their level). The student comes back and must find out the adverb by asking any of the other students to do things in the way described by the adverb, e.g. make a cup of tea, wash your face, read a book etc. After each command, he/she must guess what the adverb could be from the way the student carried out the command.

Useful games for coach trips

Alphabet grid

Everybody draws a five-by-five grid. One person begins by calling out a letter of the alphabet, the others put it anywhere they want on their grid. The next person calls out a letter which is entered on the grid, and this continues until twenty five letters have been called out. The students should aim to make as many words as possible on their grid, across and down. The one with the most words at the the end is the winner. (The same letter may be called out any number of times.)

Traffic bingo

Each player sketches a grid of three squares by three. The squares are filled in by any two-digit number. One player is the 'caller'. He/she looks out of the window of the coach and calls out the last two digits on the number plates of passing cars. Any player with that number on his/her card crosses it out, and the first to get

a line — vertically, horizontally or diagonally — is the winner.

Scavenger

Prepare a list of objects to be spotted during the journey, e.g. a dog on a lead, a traffic warden, a clergyman, somebody riding a bike, somebody pushing a pram. The first player to see one of the items scores a point. When all the objects have been spotted, the winner is the one with most points.

What's My Line

A travelling version of the old game. Someone chooses any job connected with the journey, e.g. petrol pump attendant, traffic warden, coach driver. The others then ask questions which can be answered by 'Yes', 'No', 'Sometimes' or 'I don't know'. They have twenty questions in which to discover the job.

Innings

Two players toss a coin to decide who bats first. The batsman's aim is to look on both sides of the road for pub signs which show things with legs — a run is scored for every leg, e.g. 'The Greyhound' scores 4. The batsman continues to score until the opponent spots a sign with no legs, e.g. 'The Cross Keys'. The batsman is then out and the opponent starts to bat. A match consists of an innings each.
N.B. The legs don't have to be painted on the sign.

'Legs'

One player selects a letter. The other players must write down as many objects as they can think of beginning with that letter which have legs.
Variations: arms, a head.

Some role plays

Nuclear power station

Divide the class into four groups (more if you want to write in further roles). Choose a strong student to chair the meeting. Give them the relevant background information below.
Allow ten minutes for the groups to read and develop their arguments.

Situation

There is going to be a public meeting to discuss Government plans for building a nuclear power station.

Each group gets a few minutes to put across the main points of its argument to the other groups. This is followed by a general discussion and a vote on the following motion:

A nuclear power station should be built here as soon as possible.

One of the main drawbacks of class role plays is that they tend to be dominated by the more extrovert students. The following technique often gets round this problem: start the role play by asking one member from each group to sit around the discussion table. As they begin to give their arguments, select other students from the groups to come in and replace them and continue the argument where necessary. As well as allowing everyone to speak, this also ensures that everybody listens, because the students never know when they will be called upon to pick up the threads of the previous speaker's theme.

You can also provide a surprise element by feeding in further instructions or bits of information as the role play progresses. To do this, simply jot them down on a slip of paper and give them to the student who is going to take over a role.

Roles

Government representatives. The Government wants to build a nuclear power station in one of the most beautiful and remote parts of the Yorkshire Dales. According to the latest research, our energy resources will run out·in the next fifty years. If we are to maintain our present standard of living, it is vital that we begin to use nuclear power. Research into alternative energy sources is only just beginning, therefore we cannot depend on them to provide us with our energy needs. You admit that nuclear power can be dangerous, but the Government has studied the latest report from America and believes that the plans for the new station are almost 100% safe.

Representatives of the local people and farmers. You live in one of the most beautiful areas in England. The nuclear power station will be ugly. The prices of your houses will fall; you may not even be able to sell them because no-one chooses to live near a place like this. The farmers will lose a lot of farmland. You are also afraid of leaks from the station. You have read about the Three Mile Island leak in America and you realise that even minute amounts of nuclear waste could destroy you, your children and your animals. The farmers are particularly worried about the possible effects on their livestock and crops.

Representatives of local businessmen and shopkeepers. You realise the possible dangers of building the nuclear power station but you feel that, with proper Government control, the risks are small. As far as you are concerned, the advantages outweigh the disadvantages. Building the station will provide a lot of jobs. The area has high unemployment. If people have more money to spend, their standard of living will go up and your profits should improve too.

Conservationists. You are totally against building the nuclear power station. Even with strict Government controls, the risk of leaks is high. You believe that people should accept a simpler standard of living and that the Government should be encouraging research into ways of converting safe natural resources into energy.

In the pub

Set up the following situation for the students: three or four good friends are having a night out together; they've just arrived at a pub that none of them have been to before.

Allocate roles A, B, C, D, E around the class. The students then group themselves according to the letter on their cards and discuss the language needed to deal with their situation. Visit and advise each group in turn. Then re-group the students so that each new group has persons A, B, C, D, E in it, and get them to act out the situations simultaneously. After this initial interaction, the students will know what's expected of them — their task now is to consolidate the language by discussing their roles and going through the role play again.

A. You're not drinking tonight because you're driving — order a bitter lemon. You think people who drink and drive are really stupid, as well as dangerous.

B. You heard about this pub from a friend. It's a free house and it sells a special kind of beer called 'Old Sam's', which is brewed in Yorkshire. You like to talk about beer and you always drink pints — you've had four already tonight.

C. It's your turn to buy the drinks. Try to persuade the person who orders a bitter lemon to have something stronger. The pub is old and has some interesting pictures on the wall. Ask the landlord about them.

D. You're hungry — find out what there is to eat here. When you came in, you noticed the pub sign. It was a picture of a big fat man with a red face. The pub's called 'The Jolly Farmer'. Ask the landlord where the name came from and how old the pub is.

E. You're the landlord of 'The Jolly Farmer'. It's a free house, and you and your wife have been here for ten years now. You sell very good beer but get a bit bored with people who come in and want to talk about it all the time. Your wife is a very good cook and makes excellent pies and home-made bread. You sell a lot of ploughman's lunches. You've just noticed that you've run out of bitter lemon. It's your wife's night off and you're busy — you're not in a good mood.

Mini role play

Divide the class into groups of three. Give out the following roles; the students should not look at each other's cards. Outline the general situation: they are in a restaurant, two people are customers, the third is the waiter or waitress.

In the first run-through, all the groups do the role play simultaneously. After they have discovered the content of each other's cards, they then polish up the language content and re-do it. Pick on some of the groups to act theirs out to the rest of the class.

Role A.   It's your friend's birthday. You are paying for the meal. Ask what he/she wants. Call the waiter/waitress.

Role B.   It's your birthday. Your friend is paying for the meal. Order a rare steak, chips, peas and salad. You *love* champagne.

Role C.   You are the waiter/waitress. You're very busy tonight. Take the customers' order. There is no steak tonight. Ask them what they want to drink.

Picture dictation

Here is a picture dictation to revise prepositions. Ask your students to draw the following map, or, using the same idea, substitute your local area.

Draw a road which goes from north to south. At the bottom, there's a zebra crossing. At the top, there's a crossroads with traffic lights. On the west side of the road, half way between the lights and the zebra crossing, there's a fish and chip shop. Opposite, there's a Chinese takeaway. Between the fish and chip shop and the traffic lights, there's a bank. The Chinese takeaway is between a cinema and a pub. The cinema is nearest the traffic lights. At the moment there's a bus in front of the pub. Behind the bank there's a park. There are eight trees around the park, and in the middle there's a pond. A man is standing on the west side of the park. Can he see the pub?

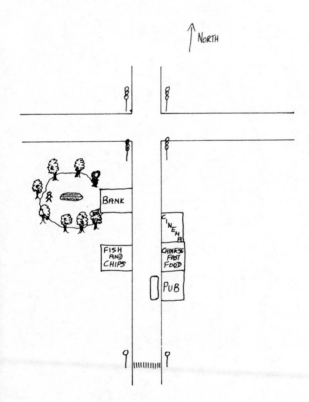

'Ordering a drink'

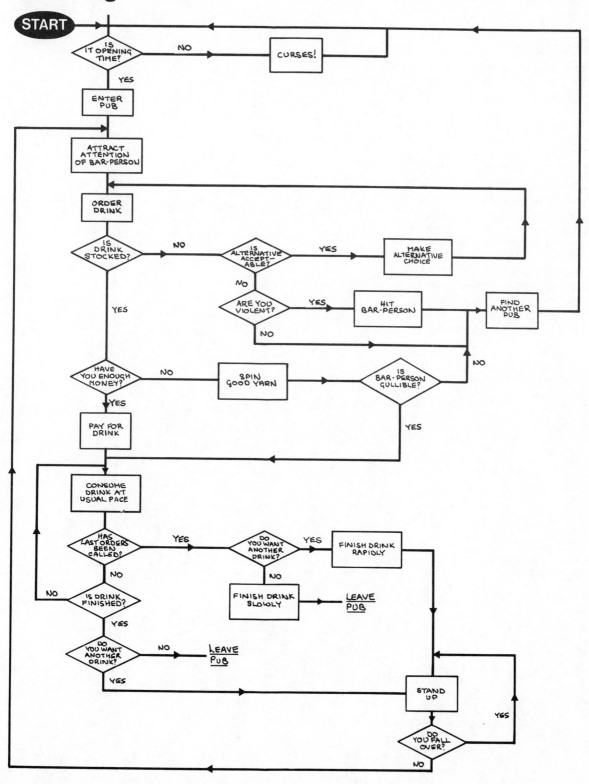